To the
Abdi's

A true family...

Rush
Limbaugh

HARREN PRESS PRESENTS

Gleanings From the Fields of Life

A Psychic's Guide to the Galaxy

BY: RUTH LORDAN

This is a work of fiction. Names, characters, places and incidents either are the product of the author's imagination or are used fictitiously. Any resemblance to actual events, locales, or persons, living or dead, is entirely coincidental. The publisher does not have any control over and does not assume responsibility for author or third-party websites or their content.

Harren Press

Copyright © 2014 Ruth Lordan

All rights reserved.
No part of this book may be reproduced, scanned, or distributed in any printed or electronic form without permission. Please do not participate in or encourage piracy of copyrighted materials in violation of the author's rights. Purchase only authorized editions.

Edited by Samantha LaFantasie
Cover Photo by Jason Wheeler
Cover Design by Chris Powell & Brant Watson

Table of Contents

INTRODUCTION: Pg 11

GLEANINGS FROM THE FIELDS OF LIFE

CHAPTER ONE: Pg 15

WHAT DOES "PSYCHIC" MEAN

CHAPTER TWO: Pg 25

THE PSYCHIC IN THE FIRST PEW

CHAPTER THREE: Pg 33

PSYCHIC POWER KEEPS YOU YOUNG

CHAPTER FOUR: Pg 47

PSYCHIC ECONOMICS

CHAPTER FIVE: Pg 63

SYNDROMES

CHAPTER SIX: Pg 89

SPIRIT ALTERING SUBSTANCES

CHAPTER SEVEN: Pg 101

HOW TO SAIL RELATION-SHIPS

CHAPTER EIGHT: Pg 121

PARENTING

CHAPTER NINE: Pg 135

WITCHING FOR A MAGIC SOLUTION

CHAPTER TEN: Pg 145

HOW TO AVOID THE RELIGIOUS RUT

CHAPTER ELEVEN: Pg 159

BALANCING IMPERFECTION

CHAPTER TWELVE: Pg 169

MOVING FORWARD AND LETTING GO

CHAPTER THIRTEEN: Pg 177

BALANCING LIFE ENERGIES

APPENDIX

Dedications:

For Spirit, which has guided me to help people and animals everywhere, this is for you. May You continue to help me keep on keeping on, grow, and prosper. Thank you to my family for recognizing and nurturing my Gifts, my many critics who strengthened me, the beaucoup folks who consulted me, Iris Perez who planted the seed of writing, Jane the artist who mystically connected me with the amazing writer/editor Jessica Freeburg, Harren Press for getting this party started and to all of you who are and will be supporting this fruit of my life's work.

INTRODUCTION:

He said, "Who are you?" And she answered, "I am Ruth, your servant."

Ruth 3:9

As a child, I was called the "little lucky piece". My family would ask me which horses to bet on, and I would predict the winners. I hadn't thought of myself as psychic until I was in college, and a friend informed me that, in fact, I was.

To me, it was just the way things were. My family accepted and encouraged my gift, as generations before me had wielded the same abilities. It wasn't something we labeled. It was simply the way some of us were. Some grandmothers knitted sweaters. My grandmother performed spiritual card readings for people in her home. For the kids who were more accustomed to the sweater-knitting grandmas, the latter might seem a bit strange. But I saw nothing strange about it because I didn't know any different.

While other children played with baby dolls and dominos, my favorite childhood toys were a priest shaman doll and copies of the Torah and the Ten

Commandments given to me by my father. My ancestors were psychically gifted and spiritually devoted (with Rabbis on both sides). It is this combination that has allowed me to develop such a strong connection between my psychic gift and my faith in God.

In my forty-three-year career as a professional psychic, palm reader, fortuneteller, and spiritual life counselor, I have been a pioneer. In the sixties, during a time when few psychics were mainstreamed, I burst onto the scene. A 25-year-old girl who went from selling her homemade oils at Renaissance Festivals to having a counter at the highest end department store in NYC where I sold my personal line of "body spirit" fragrant oils. While my high school friends became elementary school teachers, I became a cosmic elementary school teacher of sorts. Blessed with a mind that worked in ways that bewildered and captivated those around me, I shared the spiritual gift that had been born into me, and developed that gift further through study, personal mediation and innovative living.

My goal has always been to provide clients with a perspective that would give them food for thought and an experience that would "turn them on" to further growth. I seek to open the doors of perception through the heart and soul so we see in a way that enables us to achieve an outcome better suited to peace, love, and harmony for all. Quite simply, I shed light on the matters set before me.

For more than four decades, I have counseled thousands of people. My purpose in writing this book is to share with you some of the things I have learned about issues that seem to be the most prevalent matters of concern for my clients. My prayer is that my work with others may enlighten you so that you can live the life you were created to live, that your goals might be attained in an emotionally and spiritually healthy way, and that you may navigate through the road blocks of life as simply as possible. Much like Ruth who, in biblical times, gleaned in the fields, I have gleaned in the fields of life. The insight shared in this book is my contribution to the harvest.

When you reap your harvest in your field and forget a sheaf in the field, you shall not go back to get it. It shall be for the sojourner, the fatherless, and the widow, that the Lord your God may bless you in all the work of your hands.

Deuteronomy 24: 19

CHAPTER ONE

WHAT DOES "PSYCHIC" MEAN

The Holy Spirit is given to each of us in a special way. That is for the good of all. To some people the Spirit gives the message of wisdom. To others the same Spirit gives the message of knowledge. To others the same Spirit gives faith. To others that one Spirit gives gifts of healing. To others he give gives the power of miracles. To others he gives the ability to prophesy. To others he gives the ability to tell the spirits apart. To others he gives the ability to speak in different kinds of languages they had not known before. And to still others he gives the ability to explain what was said in those languages. All of the gifts are produced by one and the same Spirit. He gives them to each person, just as he decides.

1 Corinthians 12: 7-11

This is from the New Testament. It can be suggested that in the pre-Christian era and times in the Garden of Eden everyone had all of these gifts.

Even more modern cultures such as Celtic, Asian and pre-Christian cultures such as native islanders worldwide seem to be blessed with more than just one gift of the spirit.

The term "psychic" can elicit a variety of emotions from intrigue to doubt to righteous indignation. If you ask a preacher what a psychic does, you'll likely hear a verse or two about not consorting with them. However, the Bible also recounts stories of prophets who predict the future as directed by the Holy Spirit.

Psychic was not a title I ascribed to myself. It was one put upon me by others. The term psychic seems to have become a catchall label for anyone who shares spiritual gifts with others. As stated in the bible verse above, there are a variety of such gifts.

Some of us, often labeled as "intuitive", are blessed with a higher sensitivity to our gut instincts. It is important to understand that we are all inherently intuitive. That small voice that speaks to us when we are making decisions in life, the voice we sometimes choose to listen to and other times choose to ignore–that is our intuition. But intuition is highly motivated by emotions. Though it is important to listen to our intuition, we must also be capable of not allowing our instincts to be clouded by emotion.

The Bible passage above also indicates that there are those who are blessed with the ability to sense spirits and discern the good spirits from the bad. People given this ability are often tagged as "mediums". They are able to communicate with the spiritual energies around us which might include loved ones who have passed and those who are connected to us as the Divine's protective spiritual guides.

The problem with this is, mediums communicate with spirits, meaning ghosts and angels. This attracts both good and bad spiritual energies. Often times, the medium acts as a conduit and focuses on communication and making contact rather than discernment. This may be trouble as they may draw in spirits with whom they should not interact.

The Buddhists suggest, as do the Yogis, that we let the spirits come to us. The Celtics know not to attempt to enter the faery realm. Do not go seeking or asking for them. One of the 613 commandments of the Torah says this as well. When I do readings, if a spirit comes to me, I accept that. But to seek them out no matter how evolved and enlightened you are, is asking for trouble. You risk opening a realm that can bring danger.

Good spirits will come to bask in your true psychic energy and your great aura. The bad spirits will try to take it–in essence, they will feed on you if you let them.

It is possible to block the bad spirits with blessings. We can cover ourselves with our faith through communion, early baptisms, and blessing prayers. Allowing spirits to enter you is like playing Russian roulette. Let the spirits come to you: let them enjoy your aura, but do not allow them to feed on it.

When we pass, some of us are afraid because of guilt over things we have done in this life. We are afraid we may not be welcomed into the Light. Little children may simply be frightened because they do not understand. These lingering souls are called "ghosts" and are the focus of the paranormal.

These spirits need to feed on our energy in order to stay in our dimension. The guilt ridden often have demonic entities attached to them (either before death, through possession, or after death as they wander in the spirit realm). This is the inherently dangerous. If one of these lost souls attaches to you, it can cause you to develop unhealthy habits or addictions. Behavior they participated while in their physical self, that they miss in the spirit world, may be put on you.

As these spirits drain your energy, they can cause strokes, heart attacks and general bad health. I have seen this occur many times to others in the paranormal and medium worlds. If not properly protecting themselves, these people are vulnerable to the adverse effects of the energy drain.

I have often wondered how some spirits could remain on the Earth plane, while others move to Heaven. It is also curious to me that still others reincarnate. The following is my understanding of Earth and Heaven, and how they relate to reincarnation.

Spirits who pass and go to the Light, move on. If they have done amazingly well with the life they lived, they move straight to God. Most of us will go to some level of what we call "the heavens", where we will learn and progress. Some Buddhists pray for forty-nine days when a relative passes so their special prayers can guide them through the heavenly planes and they can be reincarnated.

Some spirits take years before they are reincarnated. Others earn a period of time in the heavens, and what I like to call "the bliss realms", before they come back. Spirits in the bliss realms are able to tell us things they would not have known in life because they now see from a higher plateau.

When the spirits of those who have passed come to me and give me messages for their loved ones, I have often wondered how this fits with reincarnation. During a recent channeling on a radio sports segment, it all became quite clear when I contacted the spirit of Knute Rockne, a legendary football coach of Notre Dame. Knute was famous for telling his team to "win one for the Gipper."

During the channeling, Knute told me many amazing things. One was to "use the cross." When I relayed this to the host of the radio program, the co-host of the show, Mike Morris, a former Vikings great, was amazed. He told me that was a football formation used in Knute's day. All the information Knute gave me was what he would have known in his life.

When the other host of the program, Bob Sansevere, asked Knute higher-level questions, I could not get answers. Instead, I kept seeing the vision of a baby boy. That was when it hit me: Knute had been reincarnated as a baby boy. Because his spirit was no longer residing in the bliss realms, it could only reassemble its energy into the former person and did not have the vision of a spirit residing in the higher dimensions. Once a spirit has been reincarnated and is back in the earthly dimension, it can only know what part of its previous life was.

True psychic ability is a connectedness with the Holy Spirit, through which psychic skills are used effectively. While intuition and psychic ability are connected, they are two different levels of thought. Each can be made stronger through study, practice, and the techniques I will share with you in this book. And both have great contributions in leading us down a path of contentment and joy in this life.

Psychic ability is much like our ability to sing. Almost everyone is born with a voice–some can carry a tune while others cannot. Some can affect listeners on a deeply emotional level because of the beautiful sounds created by their vocal chords. What causes one person to be tone deaf while another can sing like Patsy Cline? First, one must be born with a natural ability. Then they must develop their singing voice through discipline and vocal lessons. There are techniques that have been proven to strengthen and improve upon the natural skill that was born into a truly talented singer. Natural talent, combined with practice and consciousness, creates the vocalists who run chills up our spines and cause goose bumps to raise our flesh. The beauty of their music touches our souls. Barbara Streisand was born to sing, but her dedication to her craft made her voice legendary.

The same can be said for psychic powers. We are born with the ability to flow with them or not. Some can go very deep and touch the hearts and souls of others. Some will use their psychic gift for subjects such as business forecasting. Both are important and add value to humanity.

There are ways to develop our psychic gifts with meditation and constant practice. This can be taken a step further by refining the body as a temple with proper food, movement and rest. When all of this is combined, psychic power rings true.

I'd prefer to remove the title "psychic" all together. I was born with a spiritual gift. It was not something I asked for or even contemplated. It was simply the way that God created me. Luckily, He placed me into a family where this gift had been bestowed upon generations before me, so my parents and grandparents understood my sixth sense. No one ever told me it was wrong to use it.

They did, however, want me to be more covert with my gift. There was a fear of how other people would react to my ability. My parents wanted me to fit in, as they and their immigrant parents had sought to assimilate to their new country. Acceptance and being a contributing member of society was highly important. It has taken forty years; but then again, wandering in the desert leads us to the Promised Land.

As I grew into adulthood, I realized the power of this gift and wanted to share it. I began to see that the insight provided to me through my innate ability to perceive life through clearer eyes could help others navigate through their own lives more successfully.

If you have a talent, you should use it. If you love Biology or math, do something with that passion and ability. If you have a beautiful voice, develop it. If you were given the ability to create art, make the world a more artistically beautiful place. If you are spiritually sensitive, embrace your ability. Nurture it, grow it, and let it draw you closer to the Holy Spirit.

The ability to give clear, spiritual insight is the gift given to me by the Holy Spirit. I can either use it or pretend like it's not part of who I am. I choose to share it with others so they may find peace and joy in this lifetime as they were meant to. That is the job I was created to do.

CHAPTER TWO

THE PSYCHIC IN THE FIRST PEW

Let no one be found among you who sacrifices their son or daughter in the fire, who practices divination or sorcery, interprets omens, engages in witchcraft, or casts spells, or who is a medium or spiritist or who consults the dead. Anyone who does these things is detestable to the LORD; because of these same detestable practices the LORD your God will drive out those nations before you.

Deuteronomy 18: 10-12

You might wonder why I would start this chapter with a Bible verse that tells you people like me are detestable to the Lord. The truth is, I love the Lord. I've shared that one of my first toys was a copy of the Torah (or for non-Jewish readers, part of the Old Testament of the Bible). My ancestors were Rabbis, and holy tradition was of great importance to my family.

As a child, I could read the verse above and not attach it to myself because I never labeled myself as a medium or spiritualist. I was just a kid. I was created by God, and by his design, I possessed senses beyond the natural.

In another book of the Torah, God reiterates his distaste for divination.

Do not eat any meat with the blood still in it. Do not practice divination or seek omens.

Leviticus 19:26

Does that mean that we cannot love God and order our steaks medium-rare? I ask that only half-joking. But we cannot pick and choose which verses to which we are going to adhere. If we are to live entirely by the Christian Old Testament or the Jewish Torah, we must put as much weight on one command as we do another.

A few years ago, I met with a priest at a local Orthodox church. I had attended his church and felt in my heart that I wanted to be baptized and protected by Jesus from spirits. There I sat – a Jewish psychic, asking to be baptized. He told me I could not participate in the holy sacrament because in my profession I consort with demons. I wonder if members of the church who order their steaks medium-rare are denied the same privilege. According to Leviticus, those bloody-meat-eaters are just as detestable to God as I am.

I think it's safe to say that most of us agree it is not the internal temperature of the meat we eat that will get us into, or keep us out of, Heaven. It was not that God demanded his followers to cook their meet to well-done, so much as God wanted them to stand apart from the practices of the idol worshippers of that time.

Rest assured, I am grounded in my faith. Being denied the holy sacrament of baptism did not make me love God less. I know that He pours his blessings upon me daily. And I regularly find myself saying, "Thank you, Jesus!" Just because a man said I was not good enough in God's eyes, does not mean that Jesus sees me that way.

I count my spiritual ability as a blessing. I am employed by God to help His people get on track as so many forces derail our journey through life. Psychic power and intuition are God-given gifts. If God gives you the gift to sing, I pray you will sing for the glory of the Lord. If He has blessed you with heart for helping others, by all means, reach out to those in need in His name. Just as these gifts should be used for the good of God, so I will use my gift to reach out to my brothers and sisters and guide them on their journey down the ever-twisting path of life. It is not *my* ability—it is God's ability, bestowed upon me–shame on me, if I do not use it to further His kingdom.

If you simply look at the verses in Deuteronomy and Leviticus in passing, you may conclude that consulting with soothsayers, working with herbs and stones, using astrology to find favorable times, or consulting with ghosts and spirits, are all abominations. After many years of deep reflection, insights gained through my personal spiritual journey, and what I believe to be the voice of HaShem speaking to me, I have drawn some conclusions of my own. This is how I understand these verses, in light of my spiritual gift.

When the Torah was written, God was speaking to a culture deeply entrenched in idol worship. There is no room for idolatry when it comes to faith in God. These idol-centered religions basically allowed power-hungry kings and priests to enslave people under the pretense of faith. Their practices included such things as orgies and human sacrifice.

I found myself wondering why holy days center on the new moon and moon phases. I questioned why stones are placed on graves, and are on the breastplates of the priests, and adorn the Torah. How can herbs be used as medicines and be mentioned in Psalms, if we should not use them to heal?

My conclusion is quite simple. Nature is of God–created by God for the good of his people. Astrology, stones, herbs – they are all pieces of the puzzle God laid out for use to make sense of our surroundings. They were designed to be used for the good of mankind.

The planets are energies that have a magnetic pull. The moon affects tides. Take away the link to God—i.e. Mercury is the messenger of the gods; so when Mercury is in your sight, it rules communication. Mercury, being so close to Earth and moving quickly compared to other energy forces, can affect how we relate and communicate.

Stones have mineral properties that can affect our nervous systems. Do not use them in a ritual or proffer them to an idol. Rather use them for their benefits which the Creator, when he placed them on the Earth, intended. Nature is of God–pure and simple!

The same is true with herbs. Do not burn them as a sacrifice to an idol. In fact that may be why the Bible tells us that the odor of burning sacrificial animals was pleasing to the Lord. It distinguished the offering from the other religions which at that time were burning herbs to their gods. It is not the herbs that are unpleasing to God, but how they are being used. Use them for the healing and soothing properties that have been naturally placed within them by the Creator.

We cannot compare our present faith with the Old Testament philosophies dealing with spirit communication or prophecy. These books were written before Jesus walked the earth. When he left this world he left with us the Holy Spirit. We were meant to communicate and connect with the Holy Spirit. That was God's design.

When we open our hearts and minds to this Spirit, we gain insight and wisdom beyond our own natural ability. This is God's gift to us who believe. Do not hide away from it or view it as damnation. That would be an insult to the One who gave you the gift. Be grateful and embrace it.

Follow the way of love and eagerly desire gifts of the Spirit, especially prophecy. For anyone who speaks in a tongue does not speak to people but to God. Indeed, no one understands them; they utter mysteries by the Spirit. But the one who prophesies speaks to people for their strengthening, encouraging and comfort. Anyone who speaks in a tongue edifies themselves, but the one who prophesies edifies the church. I would like every one of you to speak in tongues, but I would rather have you prophesy. The one who prophesies is greater than the one who speaks in tongues, unless someone interprets, so that the church may be edified.

1 Corinthians 14:1-5

My advice, before seeking connection through spirit communication is to be clean and clear. There are a variety of spirits we should avoid connecting. The lost or departed souls which have not found peace and those who were never earthbound sprits to begin with, can bring negative energy into our lives if we do not approach them with caution.

Though the power of God is stronger that of the devil, we must be clean and clear within our own spirit to avoid unwanted attachments with negative spirits. If we seek only to connect with the Holy Spirit, we can avoid this all together. Anyone dealing with paranormal research must be very cautious of this fact in order to protect themselves.

We must also be aware that not every prophesy that comes out of a "religious" setting or church is from the Holy Spirit because not every person who stands within a church is spiritually holy. Look into the closets of the congregants of any given chapel and you will find someone having an affair, someone who is greedy with money, or gluttonous with food. Imperfection and sin runs deep within the walls of every religious institution. That is in part why some people are there–to seek redemption of their sins.

Sometimes, the leaders themselves live within the very corruption they preach against. I don't tell you this to downgrade religious leaders, but make you aware of the possibilities of false prophets even under the steeples of our holy places.

The psychic way is to love God and live in a clean a clear state where you can have true connection. Understand that our Creator gave us this spirit specifically for our personal well-being so we could use the gifts granted to us to draw others closer in their relationship with God. Trusting the Holy Spirit to guide us allows us to live in true faith, and this opens up the floodgate for blessings and joy.

CHAPTER THREE

PSYCHIC POWER KEEPS YOU YOUNG

For this very reason, make every effort to supplement your faith with virtue, and virtue with knowledge, and knowledge with self-control, and self-control with steadfastness, and steadfastness with godliness, and godliness with brotherly affection, and brotherly affection with love.

2 Peter 1: 5-7

The body only has so many years to walk this world before the spirit passes into the next. But ascribing to a life style that truly connects the soul with the Holy Spirit and draws one into God's Consciousness will keep the body and the spirit youthful and spry. By being spiritually connected, you become a recharging station for those around you, and when we allow the Holy Spirit to work through us, we are, in turn, recharged. There are five keys to living a spiritually connected lifestyle; clean eating, meditation, proper rest, exercise, and kindness. By incorporating these key elements into our lifestyles, we will in turn be blessed with a youthful and healthy body and soul.

Clean Eating

We can all improve our physical health and spiritual connection to self by reducing the amount of processed and man-created foods we put into our bodies. In order to be healthy, both physically and spiritually, we have to start with the basics–nutrition as fuel. We've probably heard it said, "you get what you give". This is especially true when it comes to our physical bodies. If we put quality food into our bodies, we get quality energy and wellness. One way to accomplish this is through clean eating and drinking.

The Marley Coffee folks had an ad campaign that asked, "What are you sippin' on?" in their ad campaign. This got me thinking; when drinking a beverage other than clear water, sip it. Do not chug it. Sipping will create much more awareness and mindfulness of what we are putting into our bodies, lessening the likelihood to overindulge.

Clean eating respects the physical well-being of our bodies by choosing foods that are as simple as possible. Most of us who are familiar with the Bible have heard the verse about our body being a temple.

Or do you not know that your body is a temple of the Holy Spirit who is in you, whom you have from God, and that you are not your own?

1 Corinthians 6: 19

It is important to fill our proverbial temples with foods that give us energy while not hindering our health. I call our nervous system the "fire element of our spirit". It brings in psychic power from the universe, so we should limit how much we artificially affect our nervous system with energy drinks, drugs or food.

Some foods (for example corn syrup) cause repeat cravings to a point where we almost can't get enough of them. They provide our system with a rush of sugar, and make us feel more awake or alert, but that energy cycles quickly. Once it's been used up, we crave more to replicate that feeling, but our body is not truly benefiting from that kind of empty energy as it would if we were filling it with nutritious foods that power our body and mind in a more sustainable and long term way.

If you look inside your local convenience store, the number of energy drinks you could choose from might surprise you. Energy drinks have become commonplace in our society because they work. But that artificial rush comes with a crash, and overtime, this cycle of "energy rush/energy crash" taxes our nervous system and causes permanent damage.

Although the bursts of energy provided by nutritionally empty foods and beverages can allow flashes of inspiration and some temporary energy, they come with a price. To truly live in a clean state, one needs to eat clean. This can be a challenge in today's highly processed food industry.

If in doubt about the quality of a product, take a moment to look at the label. The fewer ingredients, likely the less processed and "cleaner" it is. A sure sign that it probably doesn't fit into a lifestyle of clean eating is if the label contains words we're not sure how to pronounce.

If I purchase something I'm still not sure about, I take a small amount of the food and place it on the roof of my mouth. For a moment, I intuit and gain psychic insight as to what this food will do for me and to me. During this time I focus on the subtle physical reaction my body has to this particular food item. If I start to itch, I know that this food is a no-no for me. If my intuition tells me that a little of something will be okay, I allow myself a little. If my intuition tells me that a little will bog down my body and my mind, I stay away.

If our goal is to truly hone our psychic potential, we must begin with a strict regimen of completely clean eating. Once we've attained the state of self it doesn't make much difference what we eat from a psychic standpoint, although remaining in a state of relatively clean eating will give us clearer minds and bodies and help us maintain both physical and psychic wellbeing. Even monks, who live in a truly spiritually connected state, eat whatever they are given and often have some health issues. We would all benefit from sticking more closely to foods in their original, natural state.

Be sure to enter into clean eating in a way that works for you. Not everyone can give up favorite foods "cold turkey". In fact, trying to do so might derail your attempts to clean up your diet. My advice is to take it slow.

Eat foods that are freshly grown and cultivated by hand with love energy whenever possible. Limit your intake of foods that are high in preservatives and synthetic sugars. Grow your own produce and herbs. Even a few small pots in your windows or on a patio would do. Not only do you know exactly how they've been handled during the growing process, but you also get the added benefit of putting life energy into the world.

You likely already know it's simply better for our physical bodies to avoid the herbicides and pesticides often used in growing processes. The preservatives used to keep foods "fresh" longer, and even the linings of the cans used to store processed foods, have been linked to a variety of ailments, including cancers, autoimmune diseases and obesity.[1][2]* Such preservatives also stint the nervous system, which we need at full-power to truly tap into our psychic energy.

Pure cane sugars can actually be good for us in small amounts. However, much of the sweeteners used in our foods and diet drinks are not pure cane. These artificial sweeteners, and even pure cane sugar in excess amounts, open us up to physical and spiritual unhealthiness.

One of the rules of "black magic" is that the energy has to come from somewhere. As you can guess, it is not a positive spiritual energy that creates that kind of magic or psychic connection. It comes from negative energies. We must live in a way that does not open us up to negative energy. Clean eating is one way to ensure that we are filling our physical and spiritual selves with goodness.

A healthy body coincides with a healthy mind. A healthy mind allows for a healthy spirit. All of which leaves our proverbial temple, clean and ready for a visit from the Holy Spirit – which is the only spirit I want visiting me.

Meditation

Meditation is quite simply a time when our bodies, minds and souls can relax and rejuvenate through a moment of peaceful, quiet reflection. The emotional and physical benefits of meditation have even been documented by the world-renowned Mayo Clinic. [3]

Society has us in a constant state of forward motion. One only needs to look at how overwhelmingly busy our lives have become. Even technology has us so entwined with the world around us; we are rarely alone or unreachable. This has its advantages, but we can also find ourselves unbrokenly linked to the outside world.

And it's not just society that has us in a constant state of motion. The rules of the universe are at play as well. Earth rotates on its axis, so even when we stand perfectly still, we are still moving. We must stay mobile in order to remain in sync with the planet. Thankfully, there is meditation to get us back in tune with the natural flow.

Daily meditation allows us to grow stronger and stay strong. It allows us the necessary time to focus and recharge our bodies, minds, and souls. It is essential to take a few moments to focus solely on the self in order to truly connect with our intuition and psychic powers. The key is that self goes into Self and our individual-self aligns with the higher-self, known as Spirit.

Meditation has been practiced for thousands of years as a means of deepening spiritual connection. While this is important to making the connection between spirit and consciousness, it is also essential in overall physical and emotional wellness as a means of allowing the body and mind the time needed to rejuvenate and reconnect.

Maybe you've heard someone complain that they are so busy they might forget to breathe. We may breathe as much as we need to complete respiration to sustain blood flow in our bodies, but we often forget to breathe deeply enough to bring about deep spiritual release and connection.

Meditation is a breathing exercise. Going about our lives we breathe to survive, but not to connect with ourselves spiritually, unless we are truly in a holy place, surrounded by individuals living a truly God-Centered life. But the average person, on an average day, is simply breathing to not die. We must make a conscious effort to take breaths that reconnect our spirit with our body and mind.

Our intuition is fueled by our spiritual energy. If used carefully, it can recharge our physical energies. If used carelessly, it can deplete them. It is important to connect our spiritual energy with the Holy Spirit to avoid an unhealthy use of our psychic energy. When we connect with the Holy Spirit, using our psychic abilities can recharge us in a variety of ways–almost opening up a bubbling fountain of youth. Daily meditation allows us to connect with the Holy Spirit and reenergize with much needed spiritual fuel.

Meditation creates equanimity. We strive to become comfortable and content with ourselves and our circumstances. We do not need science to analyze or explain. In reaching this state, we have become self-in-Self.

Do this by breathing to get yourself mindful, concentrated, and aware. Feel at peace, neither up nor down. Stare at an object or person and see their impermanence. Let it flow. If at first you are drawn to the inner essence of that person or object, even better. But the main goal is to become centered in your core self.

Proper Rest

Our bodies need an adequate amount of sleep to function in a healthy way. When we allow ourselves to become deprived of that basic need, our physical bodies suffer in a variety of ways. Lack of sleep causes neurological symptoms that mimic drunkenness. It affects basic vital signs such as blood pressure, body temperature, and heart rate.[4] Harvard's School of Public Health has published research indicating that in addition to a healthy amount of evening sleep, a short nap in the afternoon can reduce the risk of heart disease by as much as 34%.[5]

In addition to the physical rest our bodies require to function properly, we also need psychic rest. I refer to this as siestas. It is when we lay down on our backs and/or sides and do focused breathing exercises. This time allows our minds to recharge and connect with our spiritual energy.

Exercise

I do not have to tell you how important daily activity is for your physical health. Research has shown that regular exercise helps control our weight, prevents some physical ailments such as heart disease, certain types of cancers, diabetes, and arthritis.[6] Just as exercise is important for our physical health, it is also essential to our spiritual health. Our spiritual well-being and clarity can be directly linked to our emotional well-being. Exercise has been proven to improve overall emotional and psychological health. The key is to sweat each day.

It is important to note that when exercising for psychic well-being, we must stay focused and centered. We need to be, what I like to call, self-in-Self. This means that it is important to not trance out or enter into a state that might be referred to as a high (such as a runner's high, dance trance, or yogi-bliss). In order to reap the full spiritual benefits of exercise, we musts remain in a state of self-in-Self.

I have surmised that it is essential to work up a sweat in the neck to activate the brown fat that is stored up our spines. Brown fat actually lends itself to increasing the rate at which we burn other fats in our bodies. [7] Achieving a good sweat in the back of the neck will aid in the healthy release of hormones and toxins.

Pre-menopausal women have "power-surges" (otherwise known as hot flashes) throughout their bodies. Those who feel their hot flashes more in the front of their bodies seem to gain stomach weight and release more stress hormones. They also tend to be diagnosed with more thyroid issues and suffer from the effects of a slowed down metabolism and depression. While those who sweat in the back of their bodies tend to get more active adrenals they tend to seem more intense and view things as being very urgent. They also tend to have a faster metabolism and lose weight.

If we are natural neck-sweaters, as some of us are prone to sweating more in other parts of bodies, we may need to really work to create the result. Dance, walk, do whatever you like to make your body sweat, but keep at it until you have worked up sweat on the back of your neck. You may also speed up the process by wearing a scarf while you exercise.

I am not a doctor. These are simply my observations based on the thousands of clients I have worked with as they seek to improve their overall well-being. I have seen that this works, time and again. I encourage you to try it, and see the results for yourself.

Beloved, I pray that in all respects you may prosper and be in good health, just as your soul prospers.

3 John 1:2

Kindness

Finally, one of the keys to living a spiritually connected life that helps maintain our youthfulness is being kind to others. Our spiritual Father has created us to love and to show compassion toward one another. When we fulfill His plan for brotherly love, we live a life that is richly blessed and we are traveling the path of true connection with the Holy Spirit.

Most important of all, continue to show deep love for each other, for love covers a multitude of sins.

1 Peter 4:8

By applying the five keys to harvesting our psychic energies, our bodies, minds, and souls maintain a youthfulness that can only be achieved by true spiritual connection with the Holy Spirit. This is how God intended for us to live, that we could enjoy life completely and fully.

Bless the LORD, O my soul, And forget none of His benefits; Who pardons all your iniquities; Who heals all your diseases; Who redeems your life from the pit; Who crowns you with loving kindness and compassion; Who satisfies your years with good things, So that your youth is renewed like the eagle.

Psalm 103: 2-5

CHAPTER FOUR

PSYCHIC ECONOMICS

Dishonest money dwindles away, but he who gathers money little by little makes it grow.

Proverbs 13:11

I know that you did not open this chapter to hear me preach about why, as people of faith, you should not set your heart on money. You likely turned to this page because you want to know how to make money and grow it. And that is what I intend to tell you. However, it is important to desire holiness and goodness *before* we desire money. Without faith, money goes away as quickly as it came.

Whoever loves money never has money enough; whoever loves wealth is never satisfied with his income. This too is meaningless.

Ecclesiastes 5:10

There's a saying I recall hearing when I lived in the South. *"Bad money spends bad..." said the Southern, bluesman.* I have found this axiom to be right on the money, so to speak.

I have seen many good intentioned, God-loving, God-fearing people settle for being poor. I find myself wondering, why, if we know God and love Him and understand that we are His children, would we assume that he would want us to settle for being broke? Doesn't it make more sense that our father would find joy in seeing us prosper so that we can use our prosperity to bless others? While some may argue that money is the root of evil, I will tell you that money is no more evil than the heart of the one who holds it.

It may seem that if someone is truly psychic, they should be rich beyond imagination. It stands to reason that we should be able to predict the winning lottery numbers, or spend a night in a Las Vegas casino and cash in with millions. I've been asked more than once, "If you're psychic, why don't you know the winning lottery numbers?" I actually got the answer to this from a devout, kind and peace-loving Muslim. He said, "Gambling is not of God so we cannot know it." Philosophizing on this from my Judeo-Christian and Hindu, Buddhist and

Native American studies, I have come to see that Gambling is part of our free will. We cannot predict it because free will is subject to change.

Although God has not graced me with the winning lottery numbers, I have personally seen the Grace of God and the convergence of Universal Harmony create wins. I had a client who told me of her relative who was diagnosed with a devastating multiple sclerosis. They had no insurance. Within two weeks of the diagnosis, they won ten million dollars in the lottery!

I have seen my clients win big in times of need like this many times. A husband and wife won more than enough at the casino just before Christmas which allowed them to pay a few bills and still give their young children a Christmas filled with all the gifts they hoped for. Another client, who was devout in her catholic faith, won big on the horse races, giving her just what she needed to pay the tuition for her daughter's catholic school.

One thing I have gleaned about gambling is that when one goes to a casino with a celebratory attitude, one can win. Going in desperate never brings good results. Though circumstances may require the grace of God to overcome, believing in the possibility of God's favor often leads to His favor being poured out on you. Those in the most desperate of circumstances who keep a positive, hopeful attitude have a better chance, sort of like Jonah in the belly of the whale. Never lose faith, and God's grace may pleasantly surprise you.

While we can find joy in simple things, it is not wrong to want financial comforts and worldly pleasures. God has given us many places to travel, many lands to explore and enjoy, especially in these times. He wants us to have enough for ourselves with some left over to share. There is no shame in having a comfortable life.

In the eight-fold path of the Buddhist faith, right livelihood is stressed and a key to acquiring great wealth is not to be attached to it. You should enjoy it, but not consider it the foundation for happiness. It is one facet of life that brings joy and contentment. There can be peace in feast and famine. But there's no reason not to seek a feast and then enjoy it, so long as we're not compromising our values in the process.

I have seen many clients do just that. Every time the fortunes they earned, as a result of compromising their values, went away. Many who I have seen marry for money have found themselves married to a poor man when their wealthy spouse lost his fortune.

We must also avoid flash-in-the-pan business. Nothing remains. You can make a quick buck, but it spends just as quickly, often leaving you with nothing to show for it.

In my work, I have counseled many individuals who struggle with money. Sometimes it is a matter of financial mismanagement. They live beyond their means or suffer from expensive addictions like gambling. But often it is not a matter of buying too many expensive toys or dinning out too many nights a week. It is simply that they need to make more money.

To obtain wealth, let's determine how we are going to go about doing so. The first step is to be clear and clean so that we can determine what we do best to make money. When dealing with clients, I find it best to sort through the things they are good at which they enjoy doing. Focus on the activities that you are self-motivated to do.

For example, if you are a young person and you enjoy sports, and find that you are practicing all the time and you are exceptionally good to the extent that you are attracting the attention of others, professional sports may be the way that you can acquire wealth. If you are someone who loves to play video games and you find yourself making your own, you may want to focus on game design. Look at the things you enjoy, which you have a natural inclination to do well at and that you actually spend time doing willingly.

Step two is to open your spiritual mind to accept that what we desire may not necessarily be our destiny or what the world wants or is willing to pay for. I have learned this truth the hard way a time or two, but my spiritual connectedness kept me from losing hope, and I still had the determination to move forward. Being in the psychic way means that we keep our mind balanced so that we never lose sight of what is possible. Our path may be redirected and wind around, but we still get home.

When an idea is right, it is right. Demand grows quickly and then we need proper management to sustain what we are building. This principal also applies to investing. With a psychic mindset, we can see what has demand and what is growing. We look beyond the one-hit flash and we are able to access the management aspect.

When clients who have been in the work force are looking for direction, I tell them to look back at their working life. Simply ask yourself, "How have I made the most money?" Go back to that. You may not return to the exact job you were doing before, but you might find that it can evolve into something just as satisfying and financially rewarding or possibly even more so.

The biggest mistake I see people make is that we often focus on trying to find our "calling" or purpose in life. If we have a "calling" – which some of us do – we will know it in childhood. You may have locked yourself away in your bedroom to write stories while your friends played tag outside. Maybe you were the entrepreneurial eight-year-old boy selling nudie magazines to other kids. Someone called to architecture and real estate construction might have been the child who preferred to build Lego constructions without the directions that came in the box. In my case, I was looking into the clouds and everywhere within and without for answers. Sitting in a natural, meditation position while I looked at what things would become. This was my calling.

For those in emotionally healthy situations, they go to school, live life, and discover the things they like and/or are good at. It may not have been their calling from childhood, but it can be nurtured and grown into a profession that brings wealth, satisfaction and a happy life.

It is not necessary to define our life's work as our "purpose". I spent many years searching for the meaning of life and the purpose of existence, until the enlightenment came to me that if it just is, let it be. It goes deeper than we see, and our soul's yearnings and longings will never be satisfied looking for purpose. That only creates a temporary high or rush of excitement in feeling like we have found the reason for being. When we are living the psychic way, we find self-within-Self. We do not need a "purpose" to define us; rather we get deeper within ourselves to "being".

Sometimes, it is karma if, as a child, we were singing on top of tables for anyone who would listen, setting up our own stores on our front lawns, inventing the next great architectural design from building blocks, or in my case, psychically reading everything and everyone around me. Then it is possible that we have a specific calling for our life. I often believe this is associated with something that we did or didn't do in our past lives, which our karma requires us to deal with it this time around.

Unfortunately, those who are raised in dysfunctional environments will find their energies caught up in survival. They do not have the luxury of focusing on their natural talents or worthy interests. Their goal is to stay whole or find a way to become whole. There are a few exceptions to this–people born into dysfunction who excel at life regardless – but that is not the normative outcome for someone born into chaos.

Often times, those who were born into dysfunction find a way to get whole within their spirit. Only after that healing can they begin to look around to see what they are good at and what they truly enjoy doing. This is when I recommend getting a college class listing and reading through it front to back. Check off each course that sounds interesting to you. Use them to narrow down your interests and then study or get jobs in those areas. Test out the line of work to see if it brings you happiness and if there is a way you can attain wealth through it.

It is also helpful to look at people around you who lead lives that ring true to the style of life you hope to live. This is not looking within, it is looking without; but it can be valuable to look beyond yourself to better understand how to achieve the goals you hold within yourself.

The best time to seek change is when you are coming from a place of power and strength, rather than one of desperation and need. Desperation and need can be highly motivating; however, they kill the vibe of success. The best time to start a business or change a career path is when you have a certain amount of financial security and can be entrepreneurial without making yourself financially ruined if your venture happens to be one of those that is not in line with what the world is willing to pay for.

Of course, you can take more chances when you are young and unencumbered. That is another kind of power and strength. Before you have commitments to a family or children may be the time to test out your dream of being an actor. If you're living in a studio apartment on a seedy street in L.A., you are only affecting yourself. But if you are unable to achieve a reasonable amount of comfort and wealth in that profession, allow yourself to find contentment in something else. Letting that passion evolve into something that can and will make you wealthy is the psychic way.

When considering business ventures, look at your idea as you might look at yourself standing in front of the mirror naked. Examine every lump and bump, freckle and scar, and ask yourself if this idea is truly something that will meet a current market demand. If not, is this idea something you are willing to invest many years into educating and training the public to like, need, and want your new product? It is easier to fill a need rather than to create one.

It is essential to keep balance so blessings can flow and grow. Often times, the way to make money is to grow where we are. I have had quite a few people come to me thinking they are in a temporary situation working at a restaurant, a retail store, or even a corporation. They are looking for their path to riches and happiness in life, but cannot see the forest through the trees. Their greatest opportunity for growth may be exactly where they are.

When one has a job with a corporate structure, the unwritten rule is to take classes and go to school when those options are offered. Bloom where you are planted if you have planted yourself in a growing organization. Perhaps it wasn't you who did the planting. God may have put you exactly where you were meant to be. Grow with it!

Once we are comfortable self-in-Self, we can do what we enjoy doing and are good at doing to get rich. The key is to be psychically clear enough to feel this with our spiritual sense.

We often make the mistake of wanting to get our money first and then work on self-in-Self. That is the road to poverty and failure. The weakened mind and body cannot perform well in the job. Take care of yourself first. Then you will have the power and strength to take care of others – whether it is your family, coworkers, the human race, the animal kingdom or spirit beings. Even the priests in ancient times cleaned and dressed before facing God. We need to get centered first, and then we can acquire wealth, and we can enjoy it in a healthy way. Begin each day by focusing and centering through exercise and meditation before you face the public and your work life.

When dealing with our finances the psychic way, we do not spend money foolishly. When one gets that windfall or big salary, it should be viewed as the last money coming in rather than the first. Don't listen to those who encourage you to spend it as quickly as you earn it. That attitude contributed to the mortgage crisis of 2008-2009.

Prosperity consciousness led people to the disillusionment that they could have it all immediately. A perfect example is the individual who signed the interest only mortgage thinking their property value would balloon. They treated their home investment as their first money. They assumed that more would come as their home value increased. Had they viewed it as their last money, they would have created equity in their home, knowing it may never be worth more than it was the moment they signed their mortgage papers.

In order to find shade in the psychic money tree, we must live in the present moment. This is where high equity is. Do not let yourself count on the future because tomorrow is not certain for anyone, not even a psychic.

This applies to careers as well. It can be very easy to get caught up in the bubble and fall into the false security that getting an advance degree (such as an MBA or doctorate) will certainly gain you better pay or a higher position on the proverbial ladder. It may, but the truth is, it may not. If the market is saturated with others holding similar degrees, that education might leave you with the same income, but more student loans to pay off.

Always keep in mind that life is impermanent and subject to change. That change may not go in the direction you are hoping it will, whether it be your house equity, stocks that are hot at the moment, a great job, or a business idea. We must see all sides, from this moment to the next.

Consider this wise statement from the late, great Dick Shapiro, founder of Jam Productions. "Anything over ten dollars is an investment." So look at everything as an investment; vacations, dinner out, even your shampoo. Are these expenditures worth putting money into. If your hair is important to your career because you are a model, then spending a little more for the better shampoo may be a good investment. But if you are struggling to pay your bills and you are buying the expensive stuff because your friends do, then it is probably not the best use of your money.

Shampoo is an example of the magic of marketing. You do not always get what you pay for. The more expensive versions of many products, including fashion, food, shelter, and even health care and pharmaceuticals, are not always better than the less expensive variant.

In the pursuit of financial well-being, we should spend time in thoughtful meditation. Be sure to live a clean life that aligns with the righteous teachings and allow God's blessings to flow. In doing so, we will find opportunities that arise which lead us toward the fruition of our dreams. With our mind cleared through meditation and prayer, we will find our intuition strengthened and our emotions controlled. This is when we can truly trust our gut because our souls are free of blurriness and we are intuitively guided by the Holy Spirit, rather than by our own heart's desires.

The God I know, love, and worship wants to bless our hard work. He wants us to be prosperous. Above all He wants us to bless one another and continue the blessing circle. Simply said, work hard and smart, bloom where you are planted, let the blessings flow, and when you have more than you need, share! Through meditation, prayer and true desire to live a God-conscious life, we can unleash riches that satisfy our spiritual and earthly needs.

Meditation Exercise

Sitting in a comfortable mediation position, take several deep cleansing breaths. Then in your mind, call to God. When your mind is cleared, envision gold coins raining down upon your head. As you do this, you will open your heart and mind to the prospects of prosperity. Doing so will allow your intuition to be open to the opportunities that will truly grow your finances.

CHAPTER FIVE

SYNDROMES

Over the years, I have read thousands of individuals from all walks of life. As different as their circumstances may be, their human experiences all hold similarities that I have seen repeated time and again. Based on these common threads, I have categorized these patterns of behavior into syndromes.

TTS: Tennis Teacher Syndrome

Generally speaking, both men and women are insecure. They tend to feel intimidated by people of the opposite sex who are on equal playing fields with them. Imagine that a man comes onto a tennis court. In this scenario, the tennis court is a metaphor for anywhere; golf course, corporate office, bar, etc. A beautiful woman catches his eye, and he sees that she can play the sport at his level.

One might think that such a fact would make the woman even more attractive to the man; however, his insecurities overpower the attraction and leave him feeling that he would have nothing to offer her. Instead he moves away from the woman, who is just as talented with a racket as he is, he is attracted to and offers lessons to a woman he finds less attractive, but who would benefit from his help. He sells himself short by assuming the woman he was truly attracted to would not be interested in him.

Because of his insecurities, he denies himself the natural attraction that drew him to the woman who was on equal ground with him, and settled for less. Often in these situations, the woman who is less skilled accepts the lessons, but ends up walking away after she has learned all she can from the man. This is in part because the natural attraction for each other was not there.

This scenario leaves everyone missing out. The woman who accepted the lesson misses out on spending that time with someone to whom she is truly attracted. The woman that the man was initially drawn to by natural attraction misses out on connecting with someone on her level. And the man ends up wasting his time and, in the end, is alone.

The key to avoiding this syndrome is for us to be self-in-Self. When we are tuned into our spirit, we can connect with others on equal ground without feeling intimidated or selling ourselves short. Then we are able to go for love without fear. In relationships, it is not what we can teach our partner or how we can improve their skills, it is simply about love. A true love connection strengthens self-in-Self which is more valuable than any lesson we could offer.

ESS: Emotional Support Syndrome

Hormones that affect our physical and emotional health regulate our bodies. Throughout our lives, hormone levels fluctuate for a variety of reasons, such as an increase or decrease in weight by ten percent, major tragedies, and age. When our glands slow down production of hormones, the adrenals take over. This is when our natural fight or flight instinct takes control, resulting in an emotional urgency.

During our twenties and early-thirties, we are focused on family and career; creating a family, nurturing the growth of our marriage and children, establishing our place in a certain field of work. Our hormones tend to regulate themselves properly during these years. Of course there are moments of hormonal fluctuation such as during pregnancies. But typically, our hormonal balance is at its prime during these years.

When the hormones begin changing, often in our late-thirties to mid-forties, all the desires we put aside in order to focus on family and career resurface within our psyche. With the slow-down of regulatory hormones and the influx of adrenaline, the urgency for "now" kicks in.

Many people find themselves seeking out ways to achieve these buried desires and goals. They seek emotional support in their pursuit of their dreams beyond their marriage and family – through reading, studying, and others who have accomplished or are working to accomplish similar goals. They often begin to feel that their spouse does not emotionally support them, and this can cause a serious rift within an otherwise stable marriage.

The key is to study yourself, read, meditate and understand that you need to control your emotions. If you are in your twenties, think deeply about what you really want to do within your lifetime, and find a way to balance those desires with family and career growth. If you are in your mid-thirties to forties and feel as if you did not get a chance to be yourself, consider two important elements:

How can you achieve that goal now? If you've always wanted to write a novel, you could join a writer's group to gather the emotional support you need to work toward that goal. If you had focused your energies on that goal in your 20's, how would life be different? You may find that when you seriously consider how your path might have been altered, you may be grateful that you chose to focus on family and/or career at that time. For example, if you had left college to pursue a career in acting, you might not have married your college sweetheart, and you may not have the wonderful children you enjoy today because you chose to hold off on that goal.

You may not have made it as an actor, but take a moment to imagine if you had. Who would you be now? If you had been a successful actor in your twenties, where would life be at forty or sixty? Would you truly have been in a better place? It's very possible that the best path for you was exactly the path you chose.

TCS: Third Child Syndrome:

I have seen this too many times to count. The woman wants a third child, but the man is content with the two children they already have. There are many factors that come into play in these situations. Often, a woman's desire to mother is so strong she feels this desire is a need rather than a want. She may be trying to fill a void within her marriage by busying herself with her children. But if a man is adamant about not wanting another child, this driving desire will eventually drive a wedge between the couple.

I have counseled many female clients who have determined that they will add that third child, whether their spouse is on board or not. Or they hound their spouse until he relents and gives her what she wants. Sadly, in 100% of these cases that I've seen, when that third child is around the age of 10, the marriage falls apart and the couple divorces.

The man may be less engaged than he should be. He might end up thinking that he did not want this extra responsibility and may consciously or unconsciously allow a thread of resentment to become entangled in his emotions where that third child is concerned. The husband may look at his life and feel slighted because of the things he was not able to do or afford because of the additional responsibilities placed upon him by a child he was not on board with adding.

The bottom line is, couples must work together and make the decision about a third child as a team. If the man truly does not want that third child, the family unit will be better off not forcing one upon him. We must be open to understanding and appreciating the input of our spouse, even if it doesn't perfectly match our own.

Society has us believing that we need to achieve *our* goals, but when we enter into a marriage, our personal goals should be merged into the family's goals. This is not about the wife being submissive. It is about both of you–you are a team–when you're psychically working together it flows because you're working on the same vibe. You do not lose yourself; you gain a bigger persona. It's not the woman being submissive or the man being in charge, but true teamwork.

Ideally, the couple creates a "family" together. It's not about self, but about family as an inclusive unit. One does not lose oneself in the marriage. One evolves into a team along with the other person. The give and take of this team has to go both ways in order for the team to function. The man must consider his wife's desires and needs just as the woman must consider her husband's.

You no longer have to do *your* thing–you do *our* thing. This synergy allows us to recreate our goals as necessary to merge our dreams and desires into one. We must apply this synergy in all aspects of our marriage, but it is especially important to consider when adding children to the family.

Marriage is a sacred state of two people working together as one for their salvation, enlightenment and life.

CDS: Cosmo Divorce Syndrome

If you scan the cover of a Cosmopolitan magazine while waiting in the check-out line at your local grocery store, you will likely see titles for articles that can make you a better lover or teach you how you can get your man to meet your needs in ten simple steps. I'm not knocking Cosmo. It is a good read. But it is not the place from which we should derive our most valuable relationship advice. Sadly, many women do just that.

Society places many unrealistic expectations into our minds through magazines, television, movies, even the lyrics of songs we sing along with on the radio. When we read an article in a magazine that tells us how life should be or could be and compare our own lives to those depicted in popular culture, we might find ourselves trying to keep up with the metaphoric Jones. It can be easy to lose sight of our true self when we compare ourselves with cultural standards.

We have all heard the complaints about the models depicted in magazines creating unrealistic body images for young women. We know that these images have been airbrushed to perfection–the bumps of cellulite in their thighs have been edited away. Yet many young women still strive to achieve the perfect body they see on the pages of their favorite magazine. We accept that this is dangerous and unhealthy, and we, as a society in general, have taken steps to move toward a more realistic depiction of physical beauty.

The same can be said for the relationship advice given in such magazines. This advice is airbrushed and edited to meet the criteria of an editor for a magazine. They are more concerned with selling copies, often with sensational taglines on the cover, than they are with improving the quality of your most precious personal relationship.

I have seen many women who take their relationship cues from popular culture and find themselves disillusioned by the advice they are given. They look for their partners to fit into a mold created for them by society rather than the mold they have created to meet their own spiritual and interpersonal needs. This often leads to feelings of failure when they are unable to attain the perfect marriage even though they have followed the article's advice to the letter.

Comparing our relationships to those depicted in magazines, movies, and quizzes can be just as dangerous as comparing our bodies with an airbrushed super-model. Sadly, many women look to magazines like Cosmopolitan, to provide them with the answers to their burning relationship questions. But who's to say the author of that article or quiz holds the same values as you. Their idea of what a healthy relationship looks like may not hold the same virtues as what your spirit desires. We must look at our relationship through our own clear eyes, rather than through the clouded eyes of a "relationship expert" who has no idea who we are, where we came from or where we hope to be.

PGICS: Peer-Group Identity Crisis Syndrome

There comes a point in our lives, when we being to question the meaning, or purpose, of life. This often occurs around the age of nineteen. Some youth have never given it much thought. They follow the flow of the stream–go to college, get a degree and travel through life based on what their peers are doing.

This is more than just keeping up with the Jones. People begin to question themselves based on their demographics in comparison to their peers. If we live in a community where the woman typically stays home with the children, yet we work outside the home, we may question our choice to do so. If our neighbors have attained a certain quality of life based on their income, but we are unable to live at the same level, we may assess ourselves as being less-than, not because we're necessarily unhappy with our standard of living, but because we don't match up with the standard of those around us.

I have seen this syndrome a lot with young adults who unknowingly base their identity on the things they think they should be doing because of what they see their peers doing. Everyone is going to college to get a degree, so they feel they must as well; however, they feel in their spirit that they should travel and explore the world instead. It could be that their path was not intended for college at that time. They could be led to travel because there is something out there for them to discover before they settle on a degree.

The part where we often mess up is when we have our lives set, and we know what we need and what we're doing, but we see friends flowing through life one way and we begin to question if we are on the right trajectory. We need to focus on our own spirit and become self-in-Self to confidently avoid the pitfall of Identity Crisis Syndrome. Being self-in-Self allows us to follow our own path confidently so we can live our best lives.

PDS: Prince/Dragon Syndrome:

Once upon a time, a beautiful princess was swept away by a heroic, young prince who slayed the dragon to win her hand in marriage. Fairytales are fun to read and even more fun to imagine being a part of. But if we look at our relationships with expectations of being saved by a prince, we may miss out on true love.

So many women actually confuse the prince with the dragon. They view a man treating them poorly as a prince proving himself, when in reality this man is a dragon who they should be running from. Yet they stay in the relationship with the expectation that this prince will eventually whisk them away to a better place. They think love has to have battles and hardships, but that is wrong.

The truth of why the prince fought to save the princess in ancient times was because he wanted her hand in marriage, not because he was so deeply in love with her; because marrying the princess meant he would inherit her kingdom. It wasn't a battle shielded in undying love, but a battle for the throne. This often repeats itself in current times when a man marries a wealthy girl, then works for her father's business.

The key is to focus on being your own protector. We do not need some prince to swoop in and save the day. A modern princess saves herself, and makes choices that divert her from needing to be saved at all. If we find ourselves in a situation that we need to get out of, we must not rely on a relationship to pull us through. Be self-in-Self–confident and secure within yourself–not relying on anyone to save you. You must slay your own dragons.

LALS: Like Attracts Like Syndrome

Dating is not so different than looking for a job. When interviewing for a position, we are hoping to find an organization that will allow us to fulfill our potential. Likewise, an employer is looking for an employee who will fill the company's needs. In a similar fashion, woman are dating with the goal of meeting a man who will allow them to meet their potential, and the man is looking for the same in a counter-mate.

If you are seeking out an athletic-minded mate, you should be athletic-minded yourself. Generally, someone who is inclined to keep their body in good physical condition is looking for a mate who is inclined to do the same. Our spirits connect with like-minded individuals. I have not found the adage about opposites attracting to hold a whole lot of truth. It does happen, but generally, our souls thrive in the company of others who are similar to us. Opposites connect like the pull of a magnet. But that type of connection tends to be less than healthy because the magnetic pull makes them cling to one another.

The logic-minded accountant can marry the free-thinking artist, but they must be prepared to overcome the obstacles of their divergent thinking. If the goal is to merge our spirit with another in a marriage relationship, it is easier to fit a square within a square than to fit a hexagon inside a triangle.

This is not to tell you to avoid relationships with those who are different than you. But you must be aware of the challenges you may face in light of your differences. We must also consider that like attracts like when we are looking for a mate and keep our expectations realistic.

If we prefer to sit on the couch and watch movies to spending time at the gym, it is not realistic to expect to find a mate who is dedicated to being in top physical shape, unless they are "for sale" because you are wealthy. This type of opposites attract connection happens all the time. Although, as I said earlier, in my experience with clients, marrying for money tends to lead to being poor. Find contentment within yourself, love yourself and allow your attraction to align with the person you are. That will allow you to build a healthy relationship because you are healthy within yourself.

DS: Dreamland Syndrome

This syndrome is simply the common mistake I see my clients make when they get caught up in an illusion of grandeur that doesn't necessarily match up with reality. We often allow ourselves to see what we want to see. We let the dream of what could be fill our souls when there is a void of tangible reality to fill it.

For example, someone might dream of owning their own business. They think about that dream, and allow their spirit to be lifted by the thought of it, yet they don't take the necessary steps to achieve it. Allow yourself to dream, but don't live in a dreamland. Make your reality what you dream and enjoy the fruits of your labor.

ICWBMSS: If Come…Will be…Maybe…Someday Syndrome

Sometimes, we are looking in one direction, but going in another. We can get so caught up in working hard that we pursue a reality that may never be. For example, if you are in your mid-thirties and hope to be a successful rapper, but have never made a successful record, the odds are that being a rap-star is not realistic.

It is possible to look at life and become so clouded by not liking the lot we see ourselves in that we miss the positive aspects. The truth is, we can take the skills we have attained in the pursuit of our dreams and apply them to transform our goals. Maybe you will never be a rap star, but if you've worked in the business trying to create your own success, you may have the skills or knowledge to be a promoter. Focus your talents on a reality that is possible rather than waiting for what may be, someday. Create your reality in the present.

Don't be swallowed up by the theory that life is hell, but Heaven will be better. Certainly, Heaven will be a perfection that we cannot fully imagine. But life should be filled with joys and successes. We live in the present so let's make it the best possible now that we can.

TS: Therapy Syndrome

We have entered a time in our society where seeing a therapist is socially acceptable. This is a good thing. We should seek counseling in times of crisis or need. And finding a good therapist is better than landing in a pot of gold at the end of a rainbow. Many therapists are good, but sometimes people go to a therapist to vent. Venting is not solving. All you do is release it for a minute. But we need relief – we need to examine it deeply – and some therapists are wonderful at this.

Other therapists may allow you to focus too much energy on venting. If you must vent, do so and then move forward; solve the problem, don't wallow in it. Let your therapist teach you techniques that will allow you to spring into a healthier state of true happiness.

A good therapist will lead you toward attaining self-in-Self. They will not allow you pay them week after week to listen to you complain about the trials and tribulations of life. Avoid being stuck in therapy syndrome by finding a therapist who will help you move toward resolution.

KCSS: Kid in a Candy Store Syndrome

This syndrome is more common in men; however, it can hold true for women as well. People who grew up as the stars of their class (i.e. captain of the football team or head cheerleader) are accustomed to having people of the opposite sex throw themselves at them. They have had their "fifteen minutes of fame" so to speak.

Fast-forward twenty-years out of high school; the man who never had his choice of girls signs up for a dating service. Suddenly he has tons of options. Because he has never had this experience before, he is like a kid in a candy store. He's not sure which to have first or if he should have more than one at a time.

A similar situation can occur for men entering nursing homes or retirement communities. They enter an environment where there are more women than men. Many of them are single because their spouses have passed away. Suddenly, he is like a whale in an ocean full of krill.

This phase is common and it's not necessarily a bad thing. Once people go through it, it is no longer about the conquest and they can focus on relationship and love. This is one reason some people struggle to commit. It is important to understand it, particularly if you are one of the krill or a piece of the candy so that you can guard yourself appropriately and not find yourself hurting because you thought it was true love when it was really just gluttony.

Understanding this phenomenon allows us to appreciate people in their ability to connect emotionally. Sometimes it's not that there is something wrong with us or even something wrong with the pairing of them with us, but rather it is the place they are in their ability to procure relationships. They must get through the phase where the many options are overwhelmingly exciting so they can move to a place where they are truly content to connect with one person.

SMS: Soul Mate Syndrome:

Everyone wants to find his or her soul mate. The idea that there is someone for everyone is cute. Like a puppy when you first bring it home from the pet store. It's soft and snuggly, but then it pees on your bed and bites your toes after chewing up your favorite shoes. Reality check–maybe you have a soul mate but you're not in a spiritual place to connect with them.

You must be firmly self-in-Self to find that kind of spiritual connection and the reality is much like the cute puppy that piddles on our floor. We are often not in the frame of spiritual awareness to connect with "the one". Most of us connect with someone who is not necessarily our true romantic soul mate, and that is ok if we understand it and do not place that expectation on them.

I say, the Tibetan woman who married all the brothers in a family got it right. The oldest brother is called father by all the children, while the others are called uncle. She was not heart set on marrying her "soul mate". She was practical in her approach to marriage. I say that half-joking. Love is important on many levels, but it is also necessary to be realistic in our expectations of our mate.

The concept of soul mate evolved into a great pick up line. It worked for a minute. I saw it many times when I lived in Los Angeles. But the 50-year-old men I saw using this line had a different 19-year-old want-to-be-starlet soul mate each night. Stop looking for some fabulous sign to point you toward your soul mate. The best way to find your soul mate is to find your own soul. And if you do not locate your soul mate on Earth, remember that our ultimate soul mate is God.

MAD: Model/Actor/Dancer Syndrome

When someone lacks the love and attention they desire, they may seek the love through fame. This is different than the person who was born to be a star—that is their destiny. But the people who want to be famous for love or in an attempt to find a way to get out of their current circumstances, may find the road to fame rutted with potholes and the final destination less than what they desired.

I witnessed this first hand a lot in the seventies and eighties. Although there are increasingly more options for young people, the lure of Hollywood and the idea that it will yield quick money and lots of it still pulls people toward seeking fame as a means of filling the hole in their heart that desires to be loved.

The answer to resolving this syndrome, like so many of the others is to love yourself. We cannot rely on others to fill our hearts with love. We must find peace and love within ourselves to accept love from anyone else.

EDS: Expression Depression Syndrome

In this syndrome, people take medications to relieve their perceived anxiety and depression, but it does not work. This is because what they are dealing with is not clinical depression. Those who are clinically depressed suffer from chemical imbalances that require medication to maintain a healthy balance in the brain. Unfortunately, many people feel depressed due to their circumstances. Medication cannot change your situation.

In this way depression is an expression of their unhappiness rather than being the cause of it. For example, a woman who is in an unhealthy marriage may suffer from a bout of depression caused by her unhappy situation. If she were to change her situation (possibly through marriage counseling), she may resolve her unhappiness. Too often, people with "expression depression" are prescribed medications when the real cure is change.

In these cases, it is important to evaluate your circumstances and determine the cause of your unhappiness and how your situation can be changed in order to alleviate feelings of perceived anxiety and depression.

Sometimes we must evaluate others around us who seem to "have it all". When we look deeply into the lives of those who appear to have what we feel we want or deserve, we more often than not see that life is no easier for them than it is for us. We must adjust our expectations.

Let's look at the woman who married young and had a family. She put her career on hold to be a mother, but now that her children are older, she questions her choice. What did she expect her life would be like at this point? If her expectations were different than her current circumstances, how can she get to where she wants to be now? These are the questions she must ask herself when she reflects on her life and overcomes her perceived depression. Drugs will not cure her sadness if it stems from uncertainty in her life. She must pinpoint the true issue and proactively change what is fueling the depressive feelings.

I find that living the Ten Commandments, the precepts of Buddhism, and the Yamas and Niyamas of Yoga, along with meditation and prayer can truly cure depression in most people. We can live our lives happier than we ever expected or imagined to be possible. The truth is that what God comes up with for us is better than what we come up with for ourselves.

What You Can Do To Prevent or Cure These Syndromes

When faced with any of these syndromes we must thoughtfully reflect on your true situation. This requires us to look beyond our own blurred vision of things, and that can be difficult to do. Through mediation and prayer, we can become truly self-in-Self, see beyond our own understanding and assess life through clearer eyes with the help of the Holy Spirit.

Meditation Exercise:

Sit down and examine the situation – what do you really want – look at the steps to get there, and see the delusions. Examine it as if examining yourself naked in front of the mirror. Look at each bump and dimple. Examine every scar and freckle. Ask yourself what you can offer to yourself and others. Ask yourself, what you have that others may want. With true self-examination, you can get to a point where you understand the why of these syndromes. Then you can be comfortable self-in-Self. That is the balancing point. See your situation for what it is and go beyond labeling it. Own it and fix it.

CHAPTER SIX

SPIRIT ALTERING SUBSTANCES

Be sober-minded; be watchful. Your adversary the devil prowls around like a roaring lion, seeking someone to devour.

1 Peter 5:8

Our feet were placed upon a path the moment our spirits entered our earthly bodies. Even if we were not specifically born with a predetermined "purpose" for our life, we were given talents and skills that would enable to us to do and achieve great things. At the same time, each of us has our own free will, which may lead us down a road pitted by potholes rather than the smoother path we began on. Sometimes we are even born into a pothole. Look at the number of children born to drug addicted mothers. Their path was rough before they even knew how to take their first step.

But potholes are a part of life. They can build character and enable us to empathize with others in a genuinely compassionate way. I am not encouraging you to jump into a pothole as your travel down your path, but I will encourage you to use your troubles to make yourself and others better. One common stumbling stone in life is substance abuse.

We have likely all been taught about the ways that drug and alcohol use and abuse can affect us physically and psychologically. I do not need to carry on about the lives lost to overdoses or drunken driving. I probably do not need to explain the permanent damage that can be wreaked upon the tissue and synapses in your brain as a result of habitual substance use or how repeated exposure to particular substances can affect the overall health of other vital organs in our bodies.

Even prescription drugs can pose potentially serious health risks. Turn on the television on any given night, and you will likely see a pharmaceutical commercial listing the side effects of a drug that you, according to them, should run out and ask your doctor to prescribe you if you suffer from the ailment it can remedy. The average prescription drug lists close to one hundred potential physical and psychological side effects. [8]

Although that sounds like a lot, the effects of drug use, both illegal and prescription, has more side effects than those listed on the information sheet handed to consumers by the pharmacist, or the lists of reasons to "just say no" to the dealer on the street corner. It is not just our mind and body affected by substances. Our spirit is altered as well.

In chapter three, I told you how to stay young the psychic way. That included healthy eating, but we put more than just food into our bodies. Even those of us who have never used illegal drugs of any kind, likely use over-the-counter drugs to alleviate aches and pains. It's not enough to eat healthy, we must be sure to keep our spirits pure with everything we put into our physical self.

Adolph Hitler is a good example of someone who made a point to fuel his body with healthy foods, but allowed the other things he put into his body to alter his spirit. Although Hitler lived on a clean, vegetarian diet, he also received doses of drugs from his personal physician including methamphetamine. [9] Mind altering drugs can open up our minds to demented spirits. It is not hard to look at the horrible things that Hitler was responsible for and acknowledge the evil that dwelled within his soul. He essentially opened the door to the devil, and the results were beyond comprehension.

None of us will likely argue that illegal drugs can invite darkness into our spirit, but what about drugs that are prescribe for us by physicians? How do they affect our soul?

There was an interesting phenomenon I noticed several years ago. I had read many people stoned on everything from acid to heroin and would see irregularities in their aura, but when I moved to Minnesota in 1987, I purchased an aura camera and began using it during readings with my clients. Most photos showed clearly defined auras of various colors around the bust of each individual. But more and more, I began to notice that some portraits showed no auras at all. As I continued my readings with these clients, I found one commonality. Each of them was using doctor prescribed anti-depressants.

I would never suggest that anyone not use the anti-depressants prescribed to them by a competent health care provider. To everything, there is a season. But it is important that we view these medications as training wheels, rather than a permanent fixture on our travels through life. There are other ways to manage our depression and anxiety.

I am not a fan of managing depression. I prefer to eliminate, cure, and heal. If you must manage I recommend exercise and a diet rich in minimally processed foods. This will help reduce the toxins within our body that may perpetuate feelings of sadness and general unhealthiness.

Bathing in Epsom salts is another great way to improve our overall spiritual, physical and mental wellbeing. The salt itself can actually reduce the amount of toxins that have leeched into our bodies, including mercury. It can reduce muscle aches and fatigue. And I think we can all attest to the therapeutic benefits of a long warm bath. Adding a scent like lavender, chamomile, or eucalyptus can increase these effects with the added benefit of aromatherapy. Some people prefer clean water. You may choose to use different fragrance cocktails at different times.

To cure or heal the depressed spirit, we must become clean and clear within ourselves. This is done by sitting down with a competent psychic or an aware therapist and directly addressing the anxiety. Acknowledge the depression or fear. Investigate all aspects of it, looking at the causes, the ineffective coping mechanisms you may have adopted and healthy approaches to making the changes necessary to eliminate or reduce the causes.

The Buddhists have Four Noble Truths, which is the best thing I have found (short of coming to me for a psychic session) to assist an individual on their path of freedom from depression and anxiety without medication.

There is suffering. Recognize that there is suffering (in this case, anxiety/depression), and then acknowledge the cause of this is desire. For example, one wants a love or a career they do not have–that is a desire, and without it they suffer.

The origin of suffering is desire. It is the want for things that causes us distress when we perceive that we do not or cannot have them.

Abandon the desire. This is done by thoroughly examining it from every angle until that desire goes away which eliminates the suffering (anxiety/depression). One of my favorite examples for this is the desire to eat a cookie. I crave something sweet, so I look at the cookie (or cigarette or job or lover) and determine what I specifically like about it. In this case it may simply be the taste or the way it makes me feel when I eat it.

Then, I consider the long-term effect of this. Is there long-term joy in eating the cookie or is it only a temporary rush of satisfaction? In the case of love, we need to look what it *really* is, not what we want it to be. With career and family issues, examine everything we know about it and study all the possibilities, including those that we are not sure about. It is amazing what clarity we gain when we realize that the issue we're facing does not have power over us. The cookie is the easiest example to use to explain this. Once you think of the long term effect (i.e., bloated feeling, extra calories, eventual weight gain, etc.) we can more easily abandon it.

The cessation of suffering is attainable. When we are anxious about our future, we must examine it so closely that we can easily see that we are living *now*, and the future that we are anxious about may never happen. Then we can clearly conceptualize the steps we need to take in order to avoid the future we fear, if at all possible. Even if the future we fear is inevitable, using this examination technique will allow us to see how we can be stronger than that which we fear.

The path to the cessation of suffering. This is accomplished through the Buddhist eightfold path which teaches how to live a life where you never create desires that cause anxiety and suffering in the first place. There is a difference between desires that are good for us and cravings. Desires that are good for us do not cause suffering but create beauty and joy in our lives and those around us.

As I said earlier, to everything there is a season. There may be moments in your life when medication can help you navigate through a difficult time. For example, if you are suddenly fired or lose loved ones in a car accident, and you become overwhelmingly sad that is not depression. But your doctor may choose to treat you with anti-anxiety or anti-depressant medications. Or you may choose to self-medicate with recreation drugs or alcohol. This likely doesn't indicate a dependence on such things. You are having a normal reaction to a life crisis, and it shall pass.

On the flip-side, if you get a great promotion, have a loving family and spouse, and a brand new home and feel like life is not worth living, this is depression which is in you. In these cases, you should manage your symptoms as prescribed by your doctor or therapist, but still work through the Four Noble Truths. Yogi sutra master Patanjali said in the Sutras, "Everything you think negatively, think the opposite." When you find yourself thinking you are unhappy, think of how you *are* happy.

Another key to happiness is goodness. Do good deeds that will enrich the lives of others. Be the best you can be at all you do. Embodying goodness leads to happiness.

When talking about illegal drugs and alcohol abuse, it is important to remember that God is of order, not chaos. Substance use invites chaos into our world, thereby blurring the orderly path we are intended to travel. In this way, drug use can actually change our destiny because when people abuse drugs or alcohol they change their personal path and ultimately affect everyone around them. .

When I was reading drug users, their future paths were unclear. They were operating on random and their spirits were subject to forces at every moment. With focus, I eventually learned to see the forces and their probable course of action, but never as clearly as I could with the non-substances users.

Addiction comes when we are trying to avoid self. Accepting self and loving self is the key to living a healthy, happy life. Meditation is the cure for the desire to escape life and or to find God through drug use.

When leaving one way of life for another (like when a young man leaves his family's farm to pursue higher education and a career in the big city), it is important to remain clean and clear. In doing so, we can learn new things and grow spiritually and emotionally in many positive ways.

However, if our mind is clouded, we may find our values compromised rather than enhanced. The rules that applied to life in our previous setting, may not apply to our new environment, and an unclear mind can lead to life altering decisions. True insight is needed at every moment in order for the new path to yield blessings rather than chaos.

It is good to seek a better life and to allow one's mind to be opened to new possibilities. But keeping our spirit unclouded by drugs is essential to achieving the ultimate rewards. There is no shame in using prescription drugs as needed, but allow them to be a temporary support as you move yourself toward peace within your spirit. You will find that peace through meditation and prayer, clean living, and ultimately connecting self-in-Self. I like to say, meditation not medication for peace of mind. That is the psychic way.

"Undisturbed calmness of mind is attained by cultivating friendliness toward the happy, compassion for the unhappy, delight in the virtuous, and indifference toward the wicked."

— *Patanjali, The Yoga Sutras of Patanjali*

CHAPTER SEVEN

HOW TO SAIL RELATION-SHIPS

I cannot claim to understand the twists and turns of love and romantic entanglements, but I have been traveling through my own journey of life for sixty-five years and working as a professional "psychic" forty-three of them. It will likely come as no surprise to you that many of my clients come to me with concerns regarding matters of the heart. Through their experiences, my psychic insight, and by virtue of coming of age myself at the height of the sexual revolution in the late 1960's and early 1970's, what follows is what I've gleaned in the fields of love.

It is my belief that Jesus brought romantic love into the world. Yes, this Jewish-Psychic, credits Jesus with love. It was Jesus who introduced the possibility of one-man-one-woman relationships. Many Hebrews of that time had multiple wives. In fact, the rich men and kings often had many wives.

In the case of the Tibetans, who were nomadic traders and hunters, the woman married all the brothers in a family. This was done because of the harsh environment and for survival of the family. The eldest is the father-figure, and called such by the children. The other husbands/brothers are called uncles.

We have evolved to a higher state of being where we, for the most part, are able to choose our partners and marry for our own reasons, rather than out of the basic need of survival. Or we choose to remain single and travel through the fields of love independently, enjoying the fruits of many loves, rather than one single love.

On Being Unmarried

Now to the unmarried and the widows I say: It is good for them to stay unmarried, as I do. But if they cannot control themselves, they should marry, for it is better to marry than to burn with passion.

Corinthians 7: 8-9

The truth is, we do not have to be married to be happy in life. In fact, the Apostle Paul advises against it in the New Testament. Not because being married is bad. Certainly, it has its benefits; but because it can cause a great deal of stress and worry.

I am not saying that to bash marriage. Marriage can be wonderful, but so can being single. Whatever category you fall into, the key to happiness is being within yourself, clean and clear, and content and at peace with your spirit. Personal happiness and contentment is essential before we can ever attempt for mutual, relational happiness and contentment.

If you happen to go through life unwed, embrace it! Find joy in yourself. Surround yourself with wonderful friends. Love relationships go beyond marriage. Fill your heart with love for yourself and others around you. It is quite possible to be a perfectly happy and contented adult who is unmarried.

We are better off to be alone than to be in a relationship and wish we were alone. Many people find their true peace and happiness in the single life. Whether they are a "rolling stone" by nature or by the circumstances of bad loves, this is the path that many walk. In an era when we can live in financial independence, we don't need to settle for an unfit spouse to provide for us. We can provide for ourselves.

I have found that many relationships have evolved out of some sort of need. Whether it be an individual's desire to become a parent or a young person's need for companionship and the fear of rejection, this is not the type of relationship that is sustainable over time. In such cases, the individuals who live in this relationships would be better off finding self-in-Self and being without a mate until they found a companion who they wanted to marry for love and not out of a perceived need.

On Marriage and Long-Term Relationships

However, each one of you also must love his wife as he loves himself, and the wife must respect her husband.

Ephesians 5:33

The key to this verse is that the man must love his wife as much as he loves himself. That means he puts her needs at the same level as his own. Her thoughts and feelings matter as much as his thoughts and feelings. When this is in balance, then the marriage is in balance.

Marriage is more than a walk-down the aisle or someone with the power-vested in them pronouncing a couple husband and wife. It is a sacred state in which two people work together as one for their salvation, enlightenment, and spiritual growth. The standard expectations of love, trust and respect are essential for the survival of a relationship and the personal growth of each individual in the partnership.

It is important to understand that no marriage is perfect. Even the relationships that last "forever," often weathered difficult storms. A successful married couple once told me they had been together thirty-seven years. Ten of those years they classified as not so good.

There are exceptions to every rule. A client once told me she was eighteen when she met her husband while he was working at a carnival. He was twelve years older than her. Three days later, they got married. Reading that scenario, one might conclude that a much older carnival worker marrying a young girl just a few days after meeting her would be a recipe for disaster; only it wasn't.

When she came to me, she was a widow in her sixties. They had been married happily for forty-plus years. It is wonderful when a relationship sails for a lifetime.

Not all relationships will weather the storms of life. Some will hit an iceberg and sink like the Titanic. Even that is not necessarily a bad thing. If, when the relationship ends, you find that you are in a better place than when it started (financially, emotionally, physically, spiritually, mentally, etc.) then the relationship was a success. Lasting forever is not the only measure to the quality of a relationship. To everything there is a season.

Over the years, I have seen unrealistic expectations wreck otherwise healthy relationships. We must see clearly past what we *want* our relationship to be and appreciate it for what it truly is. Beware of "dollhousing": when someone has a great situation (a dream house, 2.5 children, a caring spouse), but they want to plug in the perfect Barbie or Ken doll. We should not look for perfection in our significant other; we must accept their imperfections just as they must accept ours.

Sometimes women look for a wild stallion with the intention of breaking him in and housing him in a barn. They crave that kind of rugged, masculinity that comes with the free spirited type, but want to tame them into a domesticated pony. That is an unrealistic expectation.

If you like wild stallions, wonderful! Go run wild with them. That does not mean beside them through life, but for a moment before they gallop away. If you try to fence that free spirit, he will either destroy the fence you have built or become so docile that he is an entirely different animal than the one with whom you initially fell in love. Then you will likely be longing for a wild stallion to tame again.

Another common mistake I have seen over the years is that so many women fall in love with "potential" (refer back to If-Come-Will-Be-Maybe Syndrome). We may be more likely to fall victim to this syndrome if we live under the assumption that all people are good at some level.

I accept that to be true. If we are all God's creations, then we all have goodness at our true core. I would argue that even the devil began as an angel, so even his core is based in goodness. There is then, no pure evil. There are just beings not living at their core.

When we fall in love with potential, we look deeply into a prospective lover or long-term partner to see their God-self. They may not be living up to that level of potential and so we may be tempted to help lead them to a better state of being. However, unless you are spiritually gifted with the ability to heal, you cannot heal the core of others or bring them to their God-self. This is something they must seek and do for themselves.

Relationships are grounded in space time. It is true that love is love, and we are attracted to certain qualities in potential partners; but in order to make the relation-ship sail, we need the right conditions. For example, you may love bananas, but even if you're given banana trees to plant, they will not survive or bear fruit if they are not planted in the right environment. No matter how much I might love bananas, I cannot grow them in Minnesota. The same is true with people. You may love them deeply, but the conditions or time may not be right for that relationship to flourish.

That is why I say, walk into love rather than fall in love. Get to know people before you pursue a relationship with them. Understand their values. Assess how clean and clear they are spiritually. The worst possible thing we can do to ourselves within a relationship is marrying someone with the intent of changing them. You might see in them that core of goodness, but it is not your responsibility to pull that goodness to the surface.

Soul Mates

In the biblical translation, our soul mate is God. There is an idea that God created a single, perfect mate for everyone. But only those who live up to their human potential will find and keep their "soul mate". For example, a pair of young, high school sweethearts may find each other at a time in their life when they are pure and clear, living up to their potential in that they are not distracted from their true self. But often they do not build enough on the foundation of their connection and the relationship falls apart.

We can use the concept of soul mates as a blue print. But the foundation lies within the relationship we build, not the simple state of being soul mates. Harry Belafonte sang about a house being built on a weak foundation not standing. [10]

Remember that the devil is confusion. He would like to see you tripping all around the world looking for that one true love, rather than see you be the good person you have the potential to be. But that is exactly when we find our soul mates. When we at our best self.

Sometimes we are at our best, and we find our soul mate who is not at their best. That is when we must exercise the tough love of free will. We must move forward and find another.

On Divorce

But if the unbeliever leaves, let it be so. The brother or the sister is not bound in such circumstances; God has called us to live in peace.

Corinthians 7: 15

The reality is that many marriages do not sail through life. Some only sail for a short period of time. This is not ideal, but what in life is? Even God knew that divorce would occur. He even told us in the Bible that if we find ourselves divorced, He calls us to find peace in that and carry on.

My experience with my clients has shown me that divorce is hard, and I have come to believe that it is not a matter that should be taken lightly. The simple reasoning that one is "following their heart" is not the best reason to divorce.

The Lord said to Moses as follows: Speak to the Israelite people and instruct them to make for themselves fringes on the corners of their garments throughout the ages; let them attach a cord of blue to the fringe at each corner. That shall be your fringe; look at it and recall all the commandments of the Lord and observe them, so that you do not follow your heart and eyes in your lustful urge. Thus you shall be reminded to observe all My commandments and to be holy to your God. I the Lord am your God.

Numbers 15: 37-41

Before leaving a marriage, you must look at all you have built–your home, your children, the quality of your family life. Do not judge the relationship on how you feel, but on what you have built. Have you built something solid and healthy? If so, seek to repair the relationship rather than abandon it. If you were able to create a good life together, the foundation of your marriage is strong and deserves to be fully examined.

If you conclude that for true happiness and to become your best self, you must leave a marriage, be sure that you can look your children and grandchildren in the eyes and tell that you left no stone unturned. Maintain the family if you can. If you cannot, do not lose faith in love, but use what you have learned in the breakdown of one relationship to make the next better.

Through my spiritual and life counseling of individuals who have been through divorce, I believe it is best to be truthful with your children. If you keep secret the reason why your marriage failed, it is likely that they will ultimately resent you for the split whether you were at fault or not. Certainly be aware of what information your child can manage at their age. But do not sacrifice your relationship with your children for the sake of sparing the relationship with their other parent.

Being honest with your children can spare them from blaming themselves, which children often do. Children are capable of understanding more than we give them credit for. They are also open vessels of forgiveness. But if we don't allow them the opportunity to understand the truth in the separation and give them the opportunity to come to terms with the circumstances, they may very well internalize the divorce and put the burden of blame upon themselves.

If there are no children within the marriage, try to keep the financial split as simple as possible. Do not split hairs or fight over the little things for the "principle of the matter". If you are emotionally attached to the home you shared, but cannot afford to keep it on your own, let it go. Use your mind, not your heart when splitting the financials.

Finding Love Again

"Love is lovelier the second time around..."

Frank Sinatra

When old Blue Eyes sings those words, it seems that they must be true. [11] Love the second time around is more complicated but if both partners go in with eyes open, it can be true.

The fact is, sometimes we meet our soul mate the second time around. Or the third or the forth. I do suggest that if you don't find what you're looking for in a mate by the fifth marriage you stop looking and find joy within yourself as a single person.

This is where the concept of "like attracts like" comes into play. Often people are givers in their first relationships. For example, the woman who takes care of her husband and children, while the man works outside the home but offers very little help within the home. Eventually, this lifestyle may wear the woman down and she might find herself wishing for a man who would take care of her for a change.

Another example is the wealthy man who marries a trophy wife. He gives her everything she could ever want, and then she dumps him for a younger man. He made the mistake of going after someone who was not equal in his desires. She wanted to be taken care of. He wanted to have a hot wife. If he's wise, the next time he will seek a woman who is more like him. If she is in a similar financial situation with the ability to buy her own things, it is more likely to be a stable relationship.

To sail the relationship, we have to have a navigational focus centered on God and be traveling the same spiritual path. Sometimes we learn from a previously failed relationship that we put value in things that didn't really matter (i.e., money, looks, perceived potential). But the second time around, can be a smoother voyage because we can understand the true value of a relationship that is centered on soul.

By being the best person we can be and living up to our own potential we are open to a soul connection. We must also remember that like attracts like. Instead of the unhappy housewife looking for someone to take care of her for a change, she needs to focus on finding a relationship in which she and her companion take care of each other and support one another.

Not all Relationships Sail

Through my years as a psychic I have seen a trend toward five different types of relationships.

Relation-hip: It's cool and fun, but it isn't going anywhere. It's a relationship based on having a hip-good time. There's no drama and no goals for a future.

Relation-dip: You jump in and do not know what you can handle or what baggage and issues come with the person.

Relation-flips: This is when you go from one person to the next, flipping them like pancakes.

Relation-rip: These companionships cost us greatly whether monetarily, mentally, or emotionally.

Relationships: sail. They may encounter storms, but they stay afloat.

If you are looking for a long-term companion, be aware of the types of relationships that exist and seek the healthy mate who is self-in-Self, clean and clear, and ready to sail.

The Art of Relationship with an Artist

I have also seen a number of relationships that have suffered or fallen apart because one of the companions is a creative spirit. Art, of whatever nature–be it painting, sculpting, playing music, writing, inventing, etc.–is a true spirit calling. I'm talking about the true artist, not the dreamers who chase after fame or fortune. A true artist creates because they are compelled to, they create simply to create because of an internal need to do so; and if they happen to be in the right place at the right time and have the proper support to perfect their art, they may have commercial success.

I say that the piano player must first play his concerto before he makes love to his wife. Meaning, if you are an artist of any kind, that deep need must first be satisfied before you can have a successful relationship. I thank God that I am not an artist. If you are, you are and there is no denying it. Having children may be a temporary fix, but in my experience, people who give up their art fail at parenting and partnering.

For an artist to have a happy relationship it is imperative to partner with someone who understands and supports the creative spirit. They must be allowed to create simply to create, not because they are pursuing the dream of mainstream success. The dream will pursue them if the conditions are right. And if the conditions don't lend themselves to commercial recognition, in most cases the art production itself will provide the artist with a truly happy life. Because it is not the dream they chase– the art is simply a part of them that must be released.

Three Locks and Three Keys

Another concept I have developed through my decades of working as a professional psychic is the theory of three locks and three keys. Basically, there are three locks on a heart that may make an individual unable to commit to us in a relationship.

They are not available because they are in another relationship.

They are in legal struggles (on probation, in a court case, or may be involved in criminal activity for which they have not yet been caught).

They are in major debt.

The three keys to opening the heart in these situations are:

They are physically, mentally, and emotionally healthy.

You share spiritual beliefs.

You have similar lifestyles.

Activities and Meditations:

When we meet someone new, we are so involved in what we like about them, that we often fail to consider what they are attracted to in us or what they are looking for in terms of a relationship. When these new relationships begin (and periodically throughout the course of the relationship) I encourage you to stand naked in front of a mirror. Literally and figuratively ask yourself what the other person is looking for in you. What kind of relationship do they want? What do they see in you?

Cutting the Cord:

I once heard that after making love to someone six times, a cord is formed between you and that lover. If the relationship ends, the lovers must release themselves from the bond of that cord by cutting it. We do this by visualizing a silver cord between the two of you–see yourself cutting it. If you see the ends fall away from you after being cut, you were never really attached spiritually. See them falling to the ground and let it be. You can move on. If you find that the cord is still attached in your mind's eye, visualize yourself sending the ends up to God.

Dancing with their Spirit:

Another way to release the emotional energy attached to a relationship is to visualize your spirits dancing together. This works in all relationships, not just love relationships. It is necessary to release emotional stresses to live a clean, clear, and happy life and move on from the pains of failed romances, friendships or even business partnerships.

When dancing with their spirit, we surround them with loving kindness. We allow ourselves to forgive by understanding what they did and where they were coming from. We don't need to accept their action as okay, but we must have compassion for where they were mentally, emotionally, and spiritually when they hurt us.

In my experience, compassion is deeper than forgiveness and allows for true healing. We must simply release the energy. Imagine that person standing across from you. Take their hands in your own and dance with their spirit. Let go of the hurt. Feel compassion for them.

If tears come, let them come, but keep dancing. If the muscles in your throat and neck feel tight and heavy, keep dancing until you feel a release of that tension and the heaviness is replaced with a feeling of lightness. This can be difficult for some people, but when you achieve the lightness you have freed their spirit and your own. That is truly letting go.

CHAPTER EIGHT

PARENTING

To enjoy good health, to bring true happiness to one's family, to bring peace to all, one must first discipline and control one's own mind...

-Buddha

I must begin this chapter by telling you that I was not blessed with children. This was not a choice I made for myself. The blessing of a family is one I would have accepted with open arms, but that was not the path God sent me down. And so I accept the other blessings I have and do not covet those which I have not been awarded. That being said, I have had the opportunity to meet many clients who have been blessed with children, and from them, I have gleaned much, which I will share with you.

Before I share specifics about parenting with you, there is one key to wellness in life that is essential to good parenting as well. You must be centered–in other words, self-in-Self–before you can be effective at anything. Too often, I have seen my clients putting themselves last on the list of priorities as they juggle the needs of their children.

I see too many parents neglecting their own needs for personal wellness (i.e. sleep, nutrition, physical activity, mental stimulation) to accomplish the things each day that satisfy their children's needs and wants. If you leave your own cup empty, you will have nothing to pour into your children but dust and stale air. Give them the best of you by being well within yourself.

My rule in life is take care of yourself first. This means first thing in the morning, take care of you. Whether through prayer, meditation, or through conscious breathing, or even through exercise–focus and center. For married couples, you may include making love first thing in the morning because they are two together as one. After you have attended to yourself, then you can attend to others.

Happiness in life comes from within. That is why you will hear me say time and again, be self-in-Self. Center your own needs and desires before attending to those of your children or spouse and you will do better by them. It is not selfish to put your needs first; it is crucial. It truly will open your mind, heart, and energies to compassionately and effectively attend to the needs of others.

In addition, there is a trickle effect when we show care and respect for our own needs. If you are dressed in sloppy sweat clothes every day, your hair a tangled mess, your body in a state of ill health and neglect, how can you possibly command respect?

Do As I Do

Train up a child in the way he should go; even when he is old he will not depart from it.

Proverbs 22:6

I am a strong believer that early childhood experiences shape who we become as adults. Growing up where I did, on the rough streets of Chicago, my classmates and I saw junkies on the way to school. We all quickly understood that heroin was bad. We saw the effects of that bad drug by watching the prostitutes living in the rooming house across from the grade school. This was an image from my early childhood that kept me far away from the.

Humans, in general, are very visual, and this is especially true for children. But after we see something, over time, it begins to fade from our mind if we do not see it again. I suggest that you let your children see the effects of drug use and poor choices. Drive them through the skid rows and tell them why the man on the corner clutching the brown bag is sleeping on the sidewalk. Let them see it more than once.

Take a trip somewhere into a city and take the road that passes through. Let them make that connection in their minds early on and expose them to it multiple times throughout their childhood and they will make the connection–drug and alcohol abuse can ruin a person. If you live in a neighborhood where drugs are prevalent, and that could be in any socio-economic environment, you can point out the effects in your own back yard.

This is a powerful connection. One day when someone they deem as cool offers drugs or alcohol, their mind will automatically circle back to the memories of those junkies on the street corner they saw as a child.

Lead your children by example. Do not use those dreaded phrases, "because I said so" or "do as I say, not as I do." That may have worked in another generation, but it does not hold water now. Kids go to school and learn that behaviors such as smoking and obesity are bad and so will not respect a parent who lives in such ways. Teach your children how to live a good and happy life, by living your own good and happy life.

Decisions, Decisions…

The rod and reproof give wisdom, but a child left to himself brings shame to his mother.

Proverbs 29:15

There has been a common parenting technique grow in popularity over the years. It is the concept that children must be empowered by making choices for themselves. I support the concept of giving children choices, but only when appropriate and in moderation.

Toddlers are not capable of making a multitude of decisions for themselves. They're not emotionally prepared for it. Honestly, making decisions, even small ones can be a little stressful. And if you pile on one choice after another, it can become downright overwhelming!

When we allow children to make choices we know aren't the best, in a misguided attempt to allow them to learn by their mistakes, we actually teach them to make choices based on what they like, not necessarily the choice that is morally right or even healthy for them. I see this as a big problem when parents seek my counsel with concerns about a child's behavior problems. Once the child reaches adolescence, if they've been consistently allowed to make poor choices, they have developed a pattern of behavior. This isn't such a big deal whey they're choosing what they'd like to eat for dinner, but it could be life ending if they are choosing to drink and drive over calling a parent to pick them up.

Be kind to your child, and take away some of the pressures of decision making. Certainly you can allow them to choose Fruit Loops or Frosted Flakes or even which pair of shoes they would like to wear with their outfit. But limit the number of decisions they need to make, even the small ones, for their sake.

If your child becomes accustom to making all of their own decisions, you will face a power struggle of epic proportions when they become a teenager and want to make a decision that you know is unhealthy. If you put your foot down, they will likely rebel–how dare you try to tell them what to do? If you allow them to "live and learn", the consequences could be life changing (unplanned pregnancy, criminal charges, drug addiction) or life ending. I advise you to train your child from a young age to respect the decisions you make on their behalf, even if they don't understand or necessarily agree with them.

What I have gleaned over the years is that children do not discriminate on the nature of the choices they are allowed to make. It is the action of choice that they focus on. So you do not necessarily create independent thinking by allowing young children to make all of their own decisions (red cup or blue, this for dinner or that). Essentially, you create a young person who begins to believe they are entitled to the action of choosing, regardless of the nature of the choice, and rebel when they perceive their free-will is being compromised by an adult who dares to tell them what to do or what not to do.

When I Was Your Age...

It is perfectly reasonable that our parenting would be influenced by how we were parented. One thing that I've noticed throughout my years working as a professional psychic is that many of my clients' parenting rules are based on the circumstances in which they were raised. This is not necessarily a bad thing, but it is something that one should consider when determining if the parenting rules they feel are important actually apply to their current situation or location.

For example, a mother who was raised in a small town, but moved to a big city had an entirely different childhood environment to navigate. The small-town feel where everyone knows everyone no longer applies. Now she is raising children among a multitude of strangers. How might this difference affect her parenting rules?

It could cause her to be overly protective of her children and not allow them out of her sight. Her sheltered childhood may actually cause her to fear her urban surroundings.

She may be naïve and overly trusting of those around her. If she has only known people to be trustworthy (in part because you cannot get away with much in a small town with everyone knowing what you did), she may not be savvy enough to detect the potential dangers around her and her children.

The important thing is that parents live in the now. The world is ever changing. Children have smartphones and are able to text or call from anywhere at any given moment. They spend time on social media networks–making it much too easy to give out too much information or say things you would not necessarily say to someone's face. Bullies use mass messages to shame their peers, and predators troll for their next victim online. These are not concerns we had as children, but if we are parents, we must be aware of them and we must face them head-on.

Do not pretend that what worked for you as a kid will work with your own children today. Their world is not the world you grew up in. Understand it. Accept it. And parent accordingly.

Consider how much of your own behavior, attitudes and beliefs come from your early childhood development. Acknowledge that the ideas your parents and family put on you may have been misleading. They were likely well-intentioned, but that does not necessitate that they were correct. Just remember the adage, we are what our parents make us, but it is our own fault if we stay that way.

Stick a Label On It

It is good that we have become more aware of conditions that make learning more difficult for individual children; however, it seems that our society has become trigger-happy when it comes to labels. If a child is unfocused they have *attention deficit disorder (ADD)*. If they are unable to sit still we tag *hyperactivity (ADHD)* to that.

I find myself wondering, what did we do with all the children who had ADD and ADHD when I was growing up. Maybe many of them fell through the cracks. Maybe some of them learned ways to focus their attention on things that maintained their interest (for example the young man with ADD who may not do well focusing on numbers may do better with car mechanics or music).

I believe that most of these children who have been labeled with ADD and ADHD would benefit more from redirected focus than from medications that not only alter their minds but also their spirits. Find the thing that captivates them – there is always something–and let them focus on that. It seems to me that many of our past geniuses were actually children with ADD or ADHD who found their focus and made it their legacy.

We may never be able to tailor the lesson so that the child who is musically genius wants to spend hours figuring out calculus. But we can use their interests to pull them through their academic weaknesses. We may never motivate them to achieve perfect grades, but we could find contentment with their efforts and then help them find a way to use that one thing that can maintain their attention and mold it into a future career. Let's find the passion that motivates their soul, and stay away from the medication that will cloud their spirit.

This can be rewarded behavior, depending on what the focus is. I become one hundred percent focused on my readings. Take the example of someone being completely focused on cleaning the toilet. If they are one hundred percent focused on that task, they may become "super-maid". But if they are supposed to be doing other things, we might call this fixation with cleaning the toilet a disability.

For example, Asperger syndrome is really the ability to focus so much on one thing it causes us to miss other things. In some circles, that is called genius. Maybe when I am one hundred percent focused on my readings, I am actually suffering from Asperger? I often say, there are no learning disabilities, only teaching disabilities.

Parenting Through Divorce

Simply put, there is nothing simple about divorce when children are involved. If you are able to divorce your spouse before kids are in the picture, you can cut the cord and go on your merry way. But when children are involved, you are bonded for life.

My advice on parenting through a divorce is this, let go of the anger and meditate on loving kindness–for the sake of your children–for the sake of your own mental and spiritual health.

I have heard a common complaint from adults who were products of divorce that when their parents began dating again, they put all their quality time and money into their new partner. It is easy to get caught up in the rush of new love and the desire to please your new beau. But as a parent, your children must remain at the top of your priority list. Do not spend all your extra money on dinners out with your new friend and then tell your children you cannot afford a Happy Meal. Do not leave your children with your ex while you take a lavish vacation to the tropics, but tell your children you cannot afford to pay for dance classes or hockey.

The resentment will build, and rightfully so. Maintain a balance that allows your children to feel just as special or important. Do not make your children go without while they watch you woo your new love. And do not pass the buck on to your ex with comments like, "Your father is supposed to pay for that," in an attempt to justify why you should be able to fly to Jamaica with your new friend, but cannot afford to buy them a new pair of tennis shoes for track. Children keep score big time and remember it for a lifetime.

Ask yourself this–what kind of nursing home would you like to live in when you are no longer able to live on your own? I say this because when the kids grow up and come to me as an adult and complain about all they had to do without while their parents dated new partners, I tell them to look on the bright side–at least they do not need to feel obligated to put them up in the most expensive nursing home. More often than not, you get what you give. So give your children your best (as opposed to giving that new boyfriend or girlfriend your best), because one day you will be depending on them to do the same for you.

Action/Meditation:

I believe that motivating children with bonuses and raises is an excellent incentive for good grades and chores. This is, after all, how our society works. We are rewarded monetarily, materially or verbally for our good work. In addition to rewards, teach your children about consequences. For example, it is good to teach children that it is morally wrong to steal from others, but they must also understand that there are tangible consequences (such as prison time or groundings) if they do not obey the law or social rules.

Since energy goes from a parent to a child, it is essential that parents clear away negative energy and send out love and light. When a child has to block the negative energy of their parents, it weakens them spiritually. If they do not block it, then they take it in, and this poisons them.

Follow the Yogi Sage Pantanjali's advice to think the opposite. When you begin to worry, if you are clean-and-clear, meditate on love and positivity. Send out loving kindness to your children and if you are divorced do the same for their other parent. Do not allow your spirit to be darkened by anger or worry. Meditate on light and love.

CHAPTER NINE

WITCHING FOR A MAGIC SOLUTION

Psychic power has many dimensions. It is one thing to see the future–it is another thing to change it. When we do not like the way things are going or what we perceive is going to happen, we can better our circumstances. I have helped thousands see the right choices and actions to take throughout my forty-plus years as a spiritual counselor.

For most life events, this is all we need. There are choices and opportunities in life, and our efforts will bring fruits. But there are those cases where, regardless of our best efforts, we cannot seem to get it right. This is when we need a little help. The help we need lies within the energy of the universe.

There are a lot of ways to tap into this energy and they all work as long as we are able to access them. For example; Jesus' energy brings prosperity, but only to those who bond with Jesus' energy. This means they live with love and forgiveness in their hearts and minds. It is reflected in their actions at all times. Basically, you know they are Christians because they love as Jesus Christ loved–not because they tell you they are, or wear crosses, or you see them entering the front doors of the local church on Sunday mornings.

One way to achieve the quality of life we hope for is to make "prayments". This is when we sincerely pray for a better future and then we live right. When greed and hatred are in the heart, no matter how much you pray, you will not be given what you ask for. When seeking blessings through Jesus' name, be sure to make a prayment whenever something good comes your way. Simply pause and say, "Thank you, Jesus." Acknowledging the one who has poured out blessings on you will keep the blessings flowing. It works for me, and I am Jewish.

Yogis who live by the ethical and personal rules of conduct (the yamas and niyamas) and who are able to completely focus to the point of samyama (when a person completely "becomes" the energy of an object), may be able to use yogi superpowers called siddhis. The third book of the sutras of Patanjali describe these in depth.

Once in the state of samyama with an object or being, we can understand it and gain its essence while we know everything about it. For example, if we need strength, we do samyama on an elephant and get its strength. This takes a very high state of samyama. An easier example is to control appetite by doing samyama on the cavity of the throat.

I use this technique when doing readings. By deeply meditating on the person I am reading, I achieve a state of samyama. I use this to get a sense of those I am reading. I have also used this approach to enter into others' bodies, but I only do this to heal them.

This can be used negatively. Some people will use their focus to drain energy from others. These are called "energy vampires". If a true yogi does samyama on you, it will actually make you stronger because their focus is positive. However, if someone is an energy vampire, and you feel energetically drained, you can meditate to heal. If you are Christian, take communion to be refilled. Use the special mantras like prayers and blessings that correspond with your faith whether you are Muslim, Jewish, Buddhist, etc.

Using Magic

Universal energy is positive and expanding, not negative and decreasing. When we use our psychic energies to cause others to do actions against their wills, rather than just focus efforts on making ourselves or others better, we go against the universe. Since that negative energy doesn't come from the universe, it must come from within. I have seen most often that it comes from the bones and teeth of the one using the negative magic.

If we attempt to do this when we are not pure in our heart, the energy will come from us physically– often from the teeth or causing strokes or heart attacks. Remember the witch from Snow White? Disney was fairly accurate with their translation of how her hatred and jealousy caused her to do dark magic and what it took from her. I am not sharing any dark magic here, but the principle is the same. Envy comes from a dark place in your heart and if you seek out magic to satisfy your jealousies, the energy will come from your body.

If I allow my spirit to enter someone's body to heal them, I am using universal energy and creating expansion. If I enter them to make them sick or to make them do what I want them to do (against what they want), the energy comes from my own body. Giving up part of myself to change someone else doesn't seem worth it to me.

The catch is whether or not we follow the righteous paths – (whether through Christian love and forgiveness, the Ten Commandments, the Yoga Namas and Niyamas in conjunction with samadic meditation, the Buddhist precept). If you live in faith and follow the precepts of your spirituality, you can use the energy derived from Spirit to work magic. If you do not live in faith, but you choose to do magic, you will use your own energy at such a rate that you burn out before you can really have a lasting impact.

We often think of the voodoo when we think of curses or "black magic". Voodoo has its base in the African and Caribbean people who were oppressed and deeply hurt by others. What looks to be evil to others from the outside, is actually returning the hurt back to the source. This is a last resort, when reasoning and the offer of peace have been rejected and when greed and hatred have allowed no other way.

One form of magic you can use involves candles. I use votive candles. White is best, but other colors will work as well. I never use black (I like my teeth and bones). When you would like extra energy and power, and you have done everything you can (eat right, meditate, exercise, productive work) write your name on a candle three times with a Gold Eye needle. Let the candle burn down until it puts itself out. Do not blow out your luck.

While the candle is burning, it is good to meditate deeply. If you see the flame flicker or move, and there is no wind or physical explanation for it, this is a great sign that it is working. In fact "work" is the term we use for doing these things.

To see how a love is going, write female names on a pink candle three times going up with a Gold Eye needle. Do the same with male names on a blue candle. Place the pair on a plate and put three white candles between them (pic). Light them all and see what happens. Which candle moves towards the other one and which moves away? Meditate on real love and see how this affects the flow. If you don't mind losing your hair or damaging your nervous system take a wooden spoon and direct the flow where you want it to go. Oops! That's the bad stuff– never mind!

For success in business, sprinkle cinnamon and sugar outside your shop door or office or in front of your computer and say three times "money for the day." You must be open hearted and sincere.

Use honey to make someone a better person, which is a positive thing so it will not drain your even though it affects another person. Using a pencil, write the person's full name on a piece of brown paper (like from a paper shopping bag) and place it in a new jar of honey. Once the paper is fully covered with honey, close the jar, turn it upside down and put the jar in a closet for thirty days. If it seems to be working, repeat the process every thirty days.

You can use the same technique to help someone stop overdrinking by using a jar of water instead of honey. This is a perfect example of oppressed people using magic to overcome their oppressor. Many clients have come to me with husbands and wives who are abusive, cheating, etc. These people are deeply hurt. The one hurting them needs to stop. The energy for this magic comes from their pain not from their teeth, bones, hair or nervous system. A good result can be achieved and can even lead to the one they are focusing their energies on to enter treatment for an addiction that fuels their hurtful behavior.

Removing Curses

Curses are more common than people would like to think. If someone uses dark magic on you, there are ways to protect yourself. There are a few techniques I like to use to see if someone has used dark magic on me.

A simple test is to place a slice of bread on top of a flat mirror. Place the mirror, with the bread, by your bed. If on the morning of the third day, the bread is fine or has just a small amount of mold on it, then you have nothing to worry about. If the bread is especially moldy or otherwise funky, someone is sending bad energy to you. The bread is absorbing it. Flush the bread away, sending loving kindness to everyone. Continue to do this until you find the bread is no longer absorbing negative energy.

If you feel that you have been curses or possessed, there are a variety of techniques that can help remove the negative energy. Buddhists just use water in a shower or in ancient times, the flow from a waterfall. Native Americans use sage. Some Hispanic cultures bathe in Florida water.

I recommend taking a bath in kosher salt. Pat, do not rub, the salt on your skin. Likewise, pat, do not rub, when you towel off. You will feel the spiritual cleansing. This seems to be the most effective for the body to protect from curses wished by others. The shower technique used by the Buddhists works great for removing unwanted spirits. Saging works wonderfully for removing negative spiritual energy from a home.

It is foolish to think that dark magic or curses are contained to certain regions or ethnicities. We often associate black magic with Louisiana Voodoo. But curses have spread past ethnic and regional barriers into mainstream with movies and books that have glamorized such practices. There's a good chance you may never be cursed in your lifetime, but forewarned is forearmed, and if you are aware of the possibility of such things, you can protect yourself.

Vengeance

Dearly beloved, avenge not yourselves, but rather give place unto wrath; for it is written, Vengeance is mine; I will repay, sayeth the Lord.

Romans 12:19

Trust me, God can do worse punishments than I could come up with. Once a man played with my heart. I burned his underwear out of anger. But God gave better judgment than I could ever have given. The man lost millions in a business deal and engaged poor business ventures since. I cannot say that this was all because of the bad karma he acquired from hurting me, but after I gave my feelings to God and let Him deal with my pain, it seemed that the hatchet fell.

I tell you to never use your energies to bring about bad to others for several reasons. First of all, what you give into the world, the world will give back to you. We might call that karma. If you want goodness and love to come into your life, that is what you must put into the universe. If you are putting anger, hate, and negativity out there, you can be certain that is what will boomerang back into your life. It is almost like a mirror effect. We reflect that which we give.

The huna magic of Hawaii says that God needs our love to do his work. We give God the love energy through prayments. We just make suggestions with our candles and papers and herbs. To everything there is a season and when we are in tune we get the seasons right and do not waste our actions. Tuning into the right time and place lets us use our loving energy to send our needs and desires to God.

CHAPTER TEN

HOW TO AVOID THE RELIGIOUS RUT

You Pharisees and teachers of the Law of Moses are in for trouble! You're nothing but show-offs. You lock people out of the Kingdom of Heaven. You won't go in yourselves, and you keep others from going in.

Matthew 23: 13-14

There is a difference between being religious and being spiritual. Jesus was well aware of this. There are many verses in the book of Matthew that tell us exactly how He felt about the "religious" people of his time.

I know this section might ruffle the feathers of my "religious" readers, but bear with me as I explain. You might find that you are far more spiritual and less religious than you thought you were. And if you find that you identify with the religious, I pray you will find enough reasons to accept the spirituality of others while embracing your own religious beliefs.

So what do I mean by religious? When I use that term, I am referring to those who base their lives around the laws created by man to govern their spirituality. I'm not saying that all religion is bad. It has its place. And to be quite honest, some people *need* religious rules to maintain a path toward Heaven.

But the truth is, the religious rules are based on man's interpretation of a document, inspired by God, but also written by man. Man is imperfect, created by God to be so. Man never stood a chance at being perfect because he was not designed to be. So to put all your faith in the rules and regulations interpreted and defined by man seems a bit like the blind leading the blind.

I certainly believe that God inspired the Bible. I would never imply that He did not. It is a book filled with wisdom to enlighten us and lead us into a healthy relationship with Him thereby allowing us to lead the best life possible. However, its interpretations are not black and white. So was God trying to confuse us? Of course not!

The truth is, we were never intended to understand it all. That is what faith is about. Faith is knowing that there is a God who loves us even though you cannot see Him with your eyes or touch Him with your hands. Faith is finding peace in your inability to understand it all.

Personally, I love God. He is the definition of perfection. My goal is to live a life that pleases Him and radiates His love and compassion for others into the world. Others should know I am a child of God because I am different, not because I tell them so. They will see it in the way I care for those in need, in the way I love my neighbor as myself. The Lord knows they will not see me being perfect, because I simply lack the ability to do so. And in those moments, others will see me humbly accepting my imperfection and doing my best to move beyond my mistakes.

It is my personal belief that God created the Ten Commandments to protect us from ourselves. It is much like a parent telling a child not to touch the hot stove. It is not because touching the stove is a mortal sin that will damn the child to an eternity in hell. It is not even that touching the stove will make the parent love the child any less. It is simply that the parent does not want the child to hurt itself.

Parents also give their children rules that will prevent them from hurting others. For example, you might tell your children not to throw rocks at others. First of all, it will hurt the person it hits, and ultimately, cause anguish as the child suffers the resulting personal consequences–whether it be getting in trouble and having to deal with the punitive punishment that may come with hurting someone or simply the guilt of being responsible for causing another human pain.

Rules are good. They protect us from ourselves and from others. But the rules and rituals created around religions do not necessitate a relationship with God. That relationship can come with or without the rituals. Certainly, you must hold on to certain truths which allow you to live the best life you can and thereby drawing you into a closer relationship with God. But that has very little do with the standard practices of most religions.

If you are strong in your faith and love of God, you can live a good and pleasing life without the rituals of religion. If you need the rituals to keep you on the straight path toward Heaven, by all means, use them. But understand that just because that works for you, does not mean that it has to work for everyone or they are excluded from entering into eternity with God and all who love him.

The truth is, many who are strictly rooted in their religion can easily find themselves casting stones. Even though the Bible so plainly tells them not to do so they often stand in judgment of others because they are so strong in their convictions. They must maintain order by fleshing out those who break the rules. They choose to make an example out of or shame others into repentance.

That is not the way of the God I know and love. You may not live the way I would choose, but I will love you as I believe Jesus would if he were still walking this earth. Let me share with you one of my favorite stories from the Bible that illustrates what I mean so perfectly.

When Jesus went to the Mount of Olives, a group of Pharisees and other teachers of the law brought a woman to him. They stood her before Jesus, and the crowd of others who were with him, and declared that she had committed adultery and according to the Law of Moses, she should be stoned. Without answering, Jesus bent down and began writing on the ground with his finger.

When they kept on questioning him, he straightened up and said to them, "Let any one of you who is without sin be the first to throw a stone at her."

John 8:7

The crowd dispersed, one by one, until only the woman and Jesus remained. He acknowledged her sin, by telling her to go and leave her sin, but he did not condemn her for it. The lesson is, rules are good, but they weren't designed for us to beat up one another.

So often, religious people cherry pick the rules from the Bible that they will make more important than others. And often they are the principals that make us the most uncomfortable. Sex is a big one.

Strict religious folks will preach, no sex before marriage (not bad advice–you can avoid a world of hurt, unwanted pregnancy, and sexually transmitted diseases). But that rule has been so beaten into the minds of young people that they feel breaking it is a sin that will separate them from the love of God. I have seen it cause young people to marry simply because they find it too difficult to control their physical desires. I think we can all agree that this is not the best reason to be in a life-long commitment with someone. The guilt of premarital sex weighs heavily on a young person who has been told time and again that the sin of sexual impurity is a biggie in the eyes of God.

I am not encouraging young people to have promiscuous sex. I would encourage just the opposite. But why the stigma from the religious attached to this one thing? I would say, in part because we do not like to think of our children as sexual beings. Our children feel the same when it comes to thinking of their parents being sexual. It is quite simply something that we are not comfortable with. But I assure you, we are far more disturbed by the thought of sexuality than is God. After all, He is the one who created us to be sexual.

Likewise, the religious will place such a stigma on a man or woman (particularly a women) who commits the sin of adultery. But in so many of these situations, I have seen the one who finds comfort in the love of someone other than their spouse to be in a marriage where their partner is not exactly living up to the other vows spoken before God on the day of their wedding. You know the ones – to love, honor, and cherish. Those things are important to God too.

Husbands, love your wives, just as Christ loved the church and gave himself up for her.

Ephesians 5:25

I have yet to see a couple in which the woman had an affair while married to a man who loved her as God commanded him. But why do so many choose to only acknowledge the sin of not following one rule from the Bible while ignoring the other?

Live life, love God, love your brother–don't get so caught up in the rules that you beat up your brother with his sins. Even Jesus did not use the rules to persecute sinners. He simply loved them, encouraged them to turn away from their sin, and then loved them some more. If you are going to take your lead from the Bible, be like Jesus. He was much more interested in love than rituals and rules.

I tell you this not to upset you and make you question your faith. I tell you this because I want you to learn from what I have gleaned in talking openly with others. Those who come to me from strict religious backgrounds tend to carry such a burden of guilt and shame through life that they miss out on the happiness of it. They are so busy following the letters of the law, that they overlook the simplest law of them all.

"Teacher, which is the greatest commandment in the Law?" Jesus replied: "'Love the Lord your God with all your heart and with all your soul and with all your mind.' This is the first and greatest commandment. And the second is like it: 'Love your neighbor as yourself.' All the Law and the Prophets hang on these two commandments."

Matthew 22: 36-40

It is not just me who is saying this is the most important law. Jesus himself said so. If you won't take my word for it, maybe you will take His. Centuries before saw the value in love as a prerequisite for wisdom.

"A man is not called wise because he talks and talks again; but if he is peaceful, loving and fearless then he is in truth called wise."

- Buddha

The word "spiritual" has evolved in meaning over the decades. In earlier years and up through the 1960's, it referred to contacting spirits. It was, and often still is by some, frowned upon as something that distracts from the true path of righteousness. Certainly, that may be true. Because I will never achieve true righteousness, and neither will any other human being.

To me, being spiritual simply means that I love God, but I can fully love Him beyond the confines of the traditions created by religious institutions. I do not need to recite prayers or confess my sins to a priest. People who are truly strong in their faith do not need religion to have a true and loving relationship with God. Those with weaker faith or less strength within themselves to live a life of love, as God commanded, may need religion to keep them in check. I say if you need it, fine, but do not judge those who are strong enough in their love of God to not need it.

Personally, I choose to live by my Jew-Bu faith (Jewish and Buddhist). I respect the Torah and uphold the holy days. I also mediate daily and self-examine according to the Four Noble Truths. But I will acknowledge that your faith walk does not have to parallel mine to be good in the eyes of God. That is between you and Him.

It can be a beautiful thing to choose religion to keep you on the right path. I will simply advise you to be careful not to become so caught up in the rut of the rules and rituals that you become like the most religious people in Jesus' time. The Pharisees knew the laws front to back. But Jesus was unimpressed.

> *²³ You Pharisees and teachers are show-offs, and you're in for trouble! You give God a tenth of the spices from your garden, such as mint, dill, and cumin. Yet you neglect the more important matters of the Law, such as justice, mercy, and faithfulness. These are the important things you should have done, though you should not have left the others undone either. ²⁴ You blind leaders! You strain out a small fly but swallow a camel.*
>
> *Matthew 23: 23-24*

This distaste for those who believe they are more righteous than others spans other religions as well.

Buddha encouraged the Hindus to avoid the pursuit of righteousness.

Ye must leave righteous ways behind, not to speak of unrighteous ways.

- Buddha

In other words, eschew the rituals and rules that were created by man. To follow the heart of God, we must love. That love begins with loving ourselves. Only after we attend to our need for love can we let it flow to those around us.

You yourself, as much as anybody in the entire universe, deserve your love and affection.

- Buddha

Be religious if you must. Be spiritual if you can. But above all, remember the most important rules of true faith. Love God with all your heart, and love others as you love yourself. If you can abide by those rules, whether religious or spiritual, God will be pleased with you, I assure you, and you will even develop your own psychic powers.

CHAPTER ELEVEN

BALANCING IMPERFECTION

Wouldn't it be wonderful if one day we awoke to find all our flaws had vanished and we were fully perfect? I imagine most of us strive to live life in the best way we can. That is a large part of why I have written this book. I want you to achieve your best self. I would like to give you the tools I have found to be most helpful in navigating through life in the best way possible. However, no matter how hard we try to do our best, there will be moments when our imperfections shine through.

Spiritual Alchemy

A common problem I see in my clients is something I call spiritual alchemy. In this state, we do not like our life as it is. So instead of altering our perception of life, we decide to change it. We leave behind what we view as an imperfect life in pursuit of one that seems to have more to offer.

Take for example the small-town-farm girl who moves to the big city. She educates herself and leaves the pastures of her youth to pursue what she considers to be bigger and better things. She gets a high power job in the city. In reality, the change is not necessarily better, nor is it worse for that matter. It is simply different.

Environmental change may not leave her feeling as fulfilled as she hoped it would. It may leave her feeling confused and completely out of her element. She might find herself missing the quiet of her hometown. She might feel lonely even when surrounded by others because her values may not align with those around her.

This perception of not fitting in could lead to depression or even substance use and/or abuse. Or this small-town farm-girl can acknowledge her roots, find peace in the foundation of who she is, and embrace the new way of life around her. This can be a difficult process and one that requires deep reflection and self-love.

The key is to be fully self-in-Self. In this scenario, the young woman must educate herself for the sake of improving her knowledge, not necessarily to become a high-powered bigwig at a Fortune 500 company with a corner office. She may very well achieve that status, but it should not be the primary goal. The goal must be, self-improvement for the sake of self-improvement, and what follows will flow naturally from the improvements she makes.

If our primary goal is high power and great fortune, even when we achieve those things, we will not be fulfilled. We will be in a constant state of wanting more. We will never be satisfied. If the goal was simply to be educated, everything that comes with that education will be like extra gravy on our Thanksgiving mashed potatoes. We can truly appreciate and savor the fruits of labor without feeling like we are still seeking more.

We must embrace our roots, yet allow ourselves to acclimate into our environment. The sooner an individual who is in spiritual alchemy accepts that they are imperfect, their environment is imperfect, but they still choose to adapt, the sooner they will find the peace and joy in life they initially pursued.

To balance energies, we must stay strong in Self and balance our core (our roots or upbringing) with our new environment. In this way we can have our cake and eat it too, without getting fat! We can have the humble beginnings with the fabulous new life and maintain a balance of past, present and future by accepting that everything in life evolves and revolves.

Keeping a strong sense of Self allows you to keep it all in place. This is achieved by not letting our emotions rule our behavior. When we get caught up in the moment or the passion, we lose the balance between our roots and our new environment. Our footing may be thrown off and it can be difficult to recover. This is where we can fall in with bad crowds or get caught up in depression or addiction.

Self-Destructive High Expectation

Another common mistake I see my clients make is that they often place unrealistically high expectations on themselves or others. Typically these expectations come from our upbringing and can often be directly linked to the religious precepts placed upon us in our youth.

For example, if we were raised to believe that sexuality beyond the bounds of marriage is a sin and we fall into temptation and do something beyond the codes of our perceived morality, we may put undue guilt upon ourselves because we feel we have sinned against God and fallen from our faith. It is good to have moral codes. They are important to humanity. However, more important than having them is understanding that even if we don't follow them perfectly, we are still good.

Accept past actions as opportunities to learn and grow. Allow them to increase your empathy for others. The more we acknowledge and accept our imperfections, the easier it is for us to look beyond them in others and love their core being. And I believe above all else, loving one another is the greatest gift we can offer to humanity.

We can also damage relationships through unattainably high expectations that we impose on our friends or significant others. If we go into our relationships knowing that we will, at some point, be disappointed or hurt by our friend or loved one, we will be more mentally prepared to handle it when it happens. I'm not saying live in a state of waiting for people to mess up or hurt you. But do understand that disappointments within relationships are inevitable, and allow a little wiggle room for flaws and acceptance of imperfections.

My dear brothers and sisters, take note of this: Everyone should be quick to listen, slow to speak and slow to become angry.

James 1:19

If we expect perfection from anyone, including ourselves, we are destined for one disappointment after another. Strive to be better each day than you were the day before; yet accept imperfection as a natural part of being alive. Embrace it for the power it has to change and improve. Do not wallow in the squalor of imperfectness, but grow in empathy and love for others and above all for yourself.

Perfection is an unachievable goal. It is a misnomer that implies a static state. But as living creatures, we are moving energies. The concept of a perfect human is an oxymoron.

We were born into an imperfect world, and God knew before we took our first breath, each mistake we would make. The question is not, *will* you make poor choices or stumble into a pothole down the road of life? It is only a matter of *when*. The true test of life is what you do with the imperfections you encounter along the way.

Forgiveness

Jesus said, "Father, forgive them, for they do not know what they are doing." And they divided up his clothes by casting lots.

Luke 23:24

I know this may rub some people the wrong way, but I truly believe that forgiveness is an outdated concept. It is like last year's iPad. The new one is much lighter and works faster. The old version works, but the new version works even better.

To forgive, we must go back into the realm of what was done wrong to us and caused us to suffer. To forgive we look at the offender and try to understand why they inflicted the harm in the first place. With this understanding, we are able to let go. Is it really necessary to stir the mud up to the surface in order to heal? I say, no.

The better way to heel and move forward is to have a change of heart. See yourself as who you are now, in this very moment. Do not look back to the person you were when you were wronged. See the person who hurt you for who they are now, as well.

We are not the same person. They are not the same person. We do not need an affirmation ceremony to forgive, we can simply choose to let go of the vision of the old us and focus on our present energies.

If we can see that we are better off in the here and now, we do not need to focus on the past. If we are able to look at the one who hurt us and see that they are better, we can choose to see them in the light of who they are in this moment. On the other hand, if we see they are the same or worse, we will simply choose to not focus on their negative energy at all.

In the Buddhist philosophy, this is the cessation of suffering of the Third Noble Truth. Achieving this realm of happiness comes in changing your mindset away from the hurt or the perpetrator and on to positive things. You do not see yourself as a victim, therefore you do not require an apology and there is no need to go through the steps of forgiveness. That pain is simply behind you, and you are on to better things.

It is possible to balance the imperfections of life by simply accepting ourselves and others as imperfect beings. We set our sights on the achieving peace and even joy within our imperfections. We accept the truth that can find happiness in who we are in any given moment if we focus on being strong within our core being. In doing this, we move past the need to forgive for the sake of our own happiness, we move past our destructively high expectations for ourselves and others, and we prevail in our quest for true happiness in Self.

CHAPTER TWELVE

MOVING FORWARD AND LETTING GO

When we want to get over something, whether it be the pains of our past or personal addictions, we can get stuck in the quick sand of faith-based religion or psychotherapy and accept infinite resignation. We work through our problems with an understanding that in the end we are a label that fits our past choice. For example, if you were a heavy drinker, you will accept that you are an alcoholic. You may be a recovering alcoholic but in the eyes of traditional therapy, you are always an alcoholic. Or you may be a victim of childhood sexual abuse. You may be a survivor of this abuse, but you are still labeled a victim.

Why hold onto those labels? Do they help us heal? Do we move past our hurts more easily if we say, "I am a victim of abuse" or "I am a recovering addict"?

Certainly, it is good to acknowledge where we came from, but to truly heal we must let go the pain of our past, not wear it as a badge of remembrance.

We no longer have to see ourselves in the light of our past pains or mistakes. We can find joy and peace in who we are here and now.

Four Noble Truths

You must first put yourself in a place of peace so you can think clearly. We do this by becoming self-in-Self through clean and clear meditation. After we have taken the time to meditate on clean in clear out, we apply the Buddhist principal of Four Noble Truths.

The truth of suffering.

The truth of the origin of suffering.

The truth of the cessation of suffering.

The truth of the path leading to the cessation of suffering.

The truth of suffering implies that pain, anxiety and discontentment are a basic part of the human existence. We need to acknowledge that this will be part of our experience, but not dwell on it. Suffering on the physical, mental and emotional levels will be inevitable, but is not necessary for us to wallow in our sorrow.

The truth of the origin of suffering helps us understand that the root of our mental and emotional pain is our desire and hunger for things that we don't necessarily need. We crave material things and worldly pleasure that we believe will make us happy. However, true happiness comes only through being content within yourself, which is possible regardless of your human experience.

This understanding leads us to *the truth of the cessation of suffering* which allows us to follow the path toward acceptance and true self-in-Self. We can suffer. We will suffer. But we can find joy and peace in life by leaving our pain behind us as we move forward.

The truth of the path leading to the cessation of suffering requires us to acknowledge our past, but let it go. Do not define yourself by your old hurts or poor choices. Moving to a place of peace is possible, but only by accepting the inevitability of hurt and releasing the human desires that create the unquenchable thirst for things that are not necessary to achieve true transcendence.

Look at the specific pain (addiction, childhood trauma, etc.), and examine it from every angle once you are in a meditative state. Here you can see it cleanly and clearly for what it truly is because you are not controlled by emotion or pain. This is when you can let it go. You do not need an affirmation ceremony. You do not need an apology. You no longer look at the offender (whether it be someone who has hurt you or you have hurt yourself through bad decision making). The pain just drops away, completely and permanently.

Once we have let the pain drop away, we strive to apply the *fourth noble truth* and abandon the desires that cause us pain in the first place. This is the eight-fold path of right living. The goal is to never create the desire in the first place. Our only desire should be joy and beauty, the rest of our wants can be abandoned. In doing this, we will achieve true joy and through that we will find successes in life we never imagined because we are not focused on the end prize, rather it comes in on its own accord.

Once again, I encourage you to educate yourself for the benefit of being educated. Improve your physical health with the goal of being physically well. If you educate yourself solely to have huge financial success, you will never satisfy your thirst for such things. If you improve your physical wellbeing through diet and exercise with the sole goal of looking more attractive, you will never truly be content with your appearance.

You could always look better. You could always have more money. Do the things that lead you to success for the sake of doing them then reap the rewards without expectations. This is how you find true joy.

Take, for example, letting go of a past love. Get yourself into a state of clean and clear mediation and examine that love. Determine what you liked about it, which parts of those likes were based in the reality of the relationship and which aspects were more a delusion based on emotions. Look at where that person is now and would your life have been like if you had stayed with that person. Examine each detail closely. As you do this, the desire for that past love will go away.

Look at the example of the beautiful woman who desired to be a famous movie star or model, but she did not follow that path. In this case, she should examine the motivation behind the dream. Was she seeking to fill a void in her life with adoration from others because she lacked the affection she desired from her parents? Or was she truly gifted with the craft of acting and that was to be her destiny? I find if it was that later, she would have pursued it no matter the cost.

This can be applied to past hurts, failed dreams, broken relationships (romantic or family), and any other aspect of life that causes you feel less than satisfied in your current state of being. The key is to examine the desire so completely that you understand each aspect of why it was important to you. When doing this in a meditative state, these desires will literally fall away, and we can live in our present without regretting our past.

This also allows us to move beyond our past without holding anger toward those who have wronged us. When the desire and hurt melt away, there is no room for anger. It simply dissolves with the pain as our psyche lets it go.

Once we have allowed the pain to be sent away from us through meditation, we can use our meditative time to focus on sending our needs and desires to God through prayments. With clean and clear meditation and becoming self-in-Self, we will be in tune with the season of life and we will not waste our energies and actions on things that do not matter within the context of our current situation.

Tuning into the right time and place lets us use our loving energy to connect with Spirit which will lead us to where we should go. We can do this through the application of the Four Noble Truths and through the thorough examination of our failed desires and past pains. It is not complicated. It simply takes focus and enough love for ourselves that we take the time to breathe clean in and clear out until our attention can be given to the details that will allow the pains of our past to fall away. The space they occupied will then be filled with light, love, and peace.

CHAPTER THIRTEEN

BALANCING LIFE ENERGIES

For each of the hurdles I see my clients stumble over, I recommend one overriding method of resolution. That is clean and clear meditation. When we allow a little time each day to focus on ourselves, we can move past pain, achieve our financial goals without chasing after riches, sail our relationships in a healthy and fulfilling way, and connect with God without falling into the religious rut. We can overcome our own negative thought patterns and achieve a life free of depression without medication. Basically, we can do it all without worry when we are fully self-in-Self because we are connected with our own spirit, we find pleasure in simply being and follow the path of goodness which leads to true happiness.

I believe the most effective means of meditation involves three steps. I call this a "mediation parfait". Each layer deepens the level of mediation and spiritual connectedness. In addition to strengthening the mind and spirit, this parfait strengthens the physical. While I am a great fan of being in shape, I am not a fan of fad diets and exercise. This layered meditation meets all of my needs.

I recommend that each layer be done for a minimum of two minutes. Twenty minutes for each layer is optimal, but less is better than nothing. So do what you can. You will feel the results, even with ten minutes of meditation each day.

Layer One: Standing Meditation

The following six steps will guide you through a simple and effective standing meditation.

While standing with your back straight and your feet together, place your right wrist over your left wrist. This establishes your circuit of energy.

Ground your mind into your feet.

Take three deep, controlled breaths. As you inhale, think "clean". As you exhale, think "clear".

After your repetition of three "clean and clear" breaths, watch your breathing with your mind.

Strengthen the focus of your mind by thinking, "standing, standing, standing" on the inhale and exhale.

At this point, you can allow your breathing to do what it wants. Your eyes can be opened or closed. It feels more natural to close them, but is actually more strengthening to keep them open. However, either option works.

You will know that you have reached a truly meditative state when you feel no pain in your legs, the top half of your body feels light, or you see a light in your forehead that is sometimes referred to as the third eye. Once you have reached this level of mediation, you should stay in this straight position of standing meditation for no less than two minutes before moving on to the next layer.

Layer Two: Walking Mediation

The following nine steps will lead you through a basic and effective walking meditation.

Begin in the standing mediation position.

In your mind say, "standing, standing, standing."

Before moving think, "intending to walk, intending to walk, intending to walk."

Keeping your feet close to earth, placing your right foot directly in front of your left toe (heal down, ball down, then toes down). With each step think, "walking, walking, walking".

Do this for ten to fifteen paces, thinking, "walking" three times with each step.

When you complete your ten to fifteen steps, stop and think, "standing" three times.

Then think, "intending to turn" three times.

Turn in three steps (one foot and then the next, finishing with feet together equals one step). With each motion, think, "moving" (think this once for each step) for a total of three times.

Then repeat steps one through eight until you have completed at least five minutes of walking mediation. Twenty minutes would be better–an hour, better yet. But two minutes is better than nothing!

Layer Three: Sitting Mediation

You may do the following sitting on the floor, sitting on a pillow or sitting in a chair. It is completely acceptable to do this while seated at your desk at work.

Begin by crossing your right leg over your left (criss-cross). If you are sitting in a chair, you may leave your feet flat on the floor, or you may do the criss-cross position in your seat–whichever is most comfortable for you. Ideally, your back should be straight which will allow you to send the energy up to God.

With arms outstretched, palms up, imagine putting your mind in the palm of your left hand.

Turn hand over, and with your palm down, slowly move it toward your lap, flip your hand so your palm is up and opened, and let it rest on your lap.

Then put your mind in your right hand and do the same. This creates a circuit of spiritual energy.

With your posture erect, breath "clean" in and "clear" out at least three times.

When you feel the rhythm of your breathing, begin counting your breaths in your mind while focusing on "clean" in and "clear" out. Count to twenty-five.

See your breaths in your mind coming in and going out.

See your diaphragm filling up with air as you breathe in. See it contract as you breathe out. Do not contract intentionally (as in Pilates), but naturally as your body takes in and releases breath.

During sitting meditation you can focus on five things. You can choose one or all or any combination.

You can simply watch your breathing.

You can think "clean" in and "clear" out with each breath.

You can focus on the expansion and contraction of your diaphragm.

You can add counting with each breath, either before or after the "clean" in and "clear" out. Count to a minimum of twenty-five.

Focus on sending compassion out from your heat.

Do sitting mediation for a minimum of five minutes. Twenty minutes would be better, and forty to sixty minutes would be best.

If a thought comes to you, see it, but do not address it. If an insight comes to you, let it settle. You will come back to it later. You will intuitively know the difference. Insights are rare at first. You are fortunate when you get them. Appreciate them and return to them, as they are a gift.

It is not uncommon for spirits to come to you when you are in a meditative state. This is okay. Do not go with them and do not allow them to enter you. Simply send compassion to them and let them move along.

The benefits of doing all three layers together are both spiritual and physical. It will regulate the body (including metabolism and digestion). Your posture will be strengthened and improved which will strengthen your core. Your nervous system will be stimulated. Meditation will focus and strengthen your mind, muscles, bones, and organs.

On a spiritual level it will enliven your soul and allow you to focus on true joy and peace in your current situations. Through mediation you will become centered, and you will achieve self-in-Self. You can send prayments to God and give your worries and pains deep, reflective thought, allowing them to slip away with each inhalation.

I pray you will make time to strengthen your body, mind, and spirit each day through meditation. This is my greatest advice for each of my clients as they struggle through the tribulations of life. Meditate, become clean and clear, achieve a state of self-in-Self. The rest of it will fall into place from there.

If you would like to book Ruth for speaking engagements, private readings, or any other event, please contact her via her website at www.ruthlordan.com.

APPENDIX:

10 Commandments of Jewish and Christian Law

I am the Lord thy God, who brought thee out of the land of Egypt, from the house of slavery. You shall not recognize the gods of others in My presence.

Thou shalt have no other gods before Me.

Thou shalt not take the name of the Lord thy God in vain.

Remember the Sabbath day to keep it holy.

Honor thy father and thy mother.

Thou shalt not murder.

Thou shalt not commit adultery.

Thou shalt not steal.

Thou shalt not bear false witness against thy neighbor.

Thou shalt not covet anything that belongs to thy neighbor.

Buddhist Precepts

Avoid killing or harming living beings.

Avoid stealing.

Avoid sexual misconduct.

Avoid lying.

Avoid intoxication through alcohol and other drugs.

Eightfold Path of Buddhism

Right view/knowledge in regards to suffering (the Four Noble Truths): The Four Noble Truths are 1) there is suffering, 2) desire is the cause of suffering (wrong desires are those that are not joy or beauty), 3) abandon the desire and cease the suffering (walk away from it after seeing what it is), and 4) do not start to desire in the first place.

Right resolve: Freedom from sensuality, thinking of ill will, and aspiring to harmlessness.

Right speech: Avoiding slander, gossip, lying, and all forms of untrue and abusive speech.

Right actions: Adhering to the idea of non-violence (ahimsa), as well as refraining from any form of stealing or sexual impropriety.

Right livelihood: Making an honest living.

Right mental attitude or effort: Avoiding negative thoughts and emotions, such as anger, jealousy, and ill-will.

Right mindfulness: Having a clear sense of one's mental state and bodily health and feelings. Putting away greed while staying alert and mindful.

Right concentration: Using meditation to reach the highest level of enlightenment, rapture, and pleasure while maintaining control. This also leads to wisdom and insight.

Yamas and Niyamas of Yoga

Yamas: self-regulating behaviors involving our interactions with other people and the world at large

Ahimsa: nonviolence

Satya: truthfulness

Asteya: non-stealing

Brahmacharya: non-excess (often interpreted as celibacy)

Aparigraha: non-possessiveness, non-greed.

Niyamas: personal practices that relate to our inner world

Saucha: purity

Santosha: contentment

Tapas: self-discipline, training your senses

Svadhyaya: self-study, inner exploration

Ishvara Pranidhana: surrender (to God)

Further Reading

The Jewish Torah (or Old Testiment)

The Christian Bible

Abhidhamma Pitaka

The Yoga *Sutras of Patanjali*

Works Cited/Bibliography

(1) Miki Hogan. (March 8, 2013). Processed Foods Linked to Autoimmune Disease. In *Digital Journal*. Retrieved 10/2013, from http://digitaljournal.com/article/345223.

(2) Shona Botes. (September 15, 2011). Processed foods linked to increase in obesity and cancer. In *Natural News*. Retrieved 10/2013, from http://www.naturalnews.com/033578_processed_foods_cancer.html.

(3) Mayo Clinic Staff. (April 21, 2011). Meditation: A simple, fast way to reduce stress. In *Mayo Clinic*. Retrieved 10/2013, from http://www.mayoclinic.com/health/meditation/HQ01070.

(4) Brandon Peters, M.D.. (September 20, 2011). *What Are the Physical Side Effects of Sleep Deprivation?*. In About.com / Sleep Disorders. Retrieved 10/2013, from http://sleepdisorders.about.com/od/sleepandgeneralhealth/a/What-Are-The-Physical-Effects-Of-Sleep-Deprivation.htm.

(5) Noel Kingsly. (last updated June 11, 2009). National Siesta Dasy, Siesta Facts. In *SiestaAwareness.org*. Retrieved 6/14/2013, from

http://www.siestaawareness.org/pages/siesta-facts.php.

(6) Mayo Clinic Staff. (July 23, 2011). Exercise: 7 benefits of regular physical activity. In MayoClinic.com. Retrieved 10/2013, from http://www.mayoclinic.com/health/exercise/HQ01676.

(7) uncredited. (undated). Adolf Hitler, Methamphetamine Addict?. In *Amphetamines.com*. Retrieved 6/14/2013, from http://www.amphetamines.com/adolf-hitler.html.

(8) Joseph Mercola D.O.. (June 9, 2011). Average Drug Label Lists Over Whopping 70 Side Effects. In*Mercola.com* . Retrieved 7/1/2013, from http://articles.mercola.com/sites/articles/archive/2011/06/09/average-drug-label-lists-over-whopping-70-side-effects.aspx.

(9) Huffington Post Staff. (March 6, 2013). Hitler's Nazi Troops Took Crystal Meth To Stay Awake, Heinrich Böll's Letters Reveal . In HuffingtonPost.co.uk.com. Retrieved 12/1/13, from http://www.huffingtonpost.co.uk/2013/06/03/hitler-nazi-crystal-meth-heinrich-boll_n_3377033.html

(10) Burgie, Irving, and Attaway, William (1955). "Hosanna" Recorded by Harry Belefonte.

On *Calypso* [vinyl]. Webster Hall, New York City, RCA Victor Label. (1956)

(11) Cahn, Sammy (lyrics) and Van Heusen, Jimmy (music) (1960). "The Second Time Around" First recorded by Bing Cosby and Henry Mancini. On *High Time Soundtrack. [vinyl, film.]* Camden Label. (1960) "The Second Time Around" Recorded by Frank Sinatra. On *Sinatra's Sinatra* [vinyl]. Hollywood, Reprise Label. (1963)